The Independent Entertainer:

How to Be a Successful Clown, Juggler, Mime, Magician or Puppeteer

Happy Jack Feder

Prentice-Hall, Inc., Englewood Cliffs, New Jersey 07632

For Dick Bastian, a good friend,
and Dr. James Naiden, a good instructor

The Independent Entertainer: How to Be a Successful Clown, Juggler, Mime, Magician or Puppeteer by Happy Jack Feder

Copyright © 1982 by Happy Jack Feder

Printed in the United States of America

Prentice-Hall International, Inc., London/Prentice-Hall of Australia, Pty. Ltd., Sydney/Prentice-Hall of Canada, Ltd., Toronto/Prentice-Hall of India Private Ltd., New Delhi/Prentice-Hall of Japan, Inc., Tokyo/Prentice-Hall of Southeast Asia Pte. Ltd., Singapore/Whitehall Books Limited, Wellington, New Zealand

10 9 8 7 6 5 4 3 2 1

Library of Congress Cataloging in Publication Data

Feder, Happy Jack.
    The independent entertainer.

    Includes index.
    1. Performing arts—Vocational guidance.
I. Title.
PN1580.F4   791'.023'73   81-15352
ISBN 0-13-456772-2   AACR2
ISBN 0-13-456764-1 {PBK}

Introduction

The Goal

Things are humming right along on the corner of Seventh and Main. Businessmen streak by, clutching their briefcases and impatiently slowing for pedestrians and cars. In groups of twos and threes, young teenage girls are strolling as they chat and look for other friends. Shuffling carefully, an old woman leans on her worn out cane and clutches her small bag of groceries tightly. Young guys bounce and be-bop around the corner with hands in pockets, looking for those groups of girls. A mother leans over a baby carriage to snap a few ineffective orders to her crying child. A car horn beeps. The signal flashes WALK. A truck roars into gear.

It is a typically busy afternoon. Everyone walks in his or her own little path with no time for any side trips.

Until ...

Until *he* comes along. Him. That guy in those loose, baggy black pants and that tight white shirt. The guy with the white grease paint smeared all over his face. *That* guy. Him. The mime.

He stops on the corner, tosses a little hat on the sidewalk, and begins his performance. It doesn't seem to matter to him that no audience, no stage, no cameras are present.

He begins his performance with an attempt to inflate an invisible balloon.

The first person to continue walking past the mime makes the performer feel as visible as the balloon. The pedestrian doesn't even turn his head. But does the mime let that stop the show or slow his enthusiasm? No way. He begins to puff air with increased energy.

Those teenage girls are approaching now—slowing, pointing, giggling—stopping! *An audience!* This encourages others to stop and watch. A man carrying a briefcase slows down and chuckles, drops something into the hat, and walks off, still smiling. The old woman with the groceries stops her shuffling and bends her stiffened neck up to watch. The mime ties an imaginary string around the end of the imaginary balloon and hands it to the old woman. The rapidly growing crowd applauds her, and she blushes. The performance is off to a good start.

Toward the end of the day, after the crowds have thinned, the mime picks up his hat, transfers the fistfuls of change to his pockets, and makes his way home—quickly. Is he afraid of being robbed? Perhaps. Mostly, he's hurrying to get home and change into his clown costume for his weekly show at the pizza parlor.

The heavy sag of coins in his pockets, muses the mime, is almost, but not quite, as rewarding as all the smiles he has put on the unsuspecting faces—especially that of the old woman who shuffled away carrying the invisible balloon. He'll pack that special memory away with all the others that are unique to the type of artist he is—the Independent Entertainer. He works by and for himself, whenever and wherever he pleases—on street corners, in pizza parlors, at laundromats, banquets, birthday parties, you name it. His stage is wherever his two feet are touching down.

"Sounds Great! Where Do I Sign Up?"

Ah, for the life of a free, Independent Entertainer, indeed! Sounds great, doesn't it? You can put on your little mime shows on street corners, do clown shows at pizza parlors, a quick juggling performance at the local Elks Club annual picnic, a full-length puppet show at the community center, or magic tricks for a line of bored people waiting to get into a movie theater.

I'm sure you can think of all kinds of interesting and fun things to do on an independent level. But haven't you ever wondered why you so rarely see Independent Entertainment performed? Or why, even though you'd like nothing better than to walk into a room dressed as a clown and do silly things to make people laugh, you never seem to get much beyond the thought?

"Hard Work? Just to Be a Clown and Act Silly?"

To become even moderately successful as a mime, puppeteer, magician, clown, juggler—or whatever else—requires an exceptionally large amount of self-motivation. Your commitment must be honest and complete.

Except for the number of competitors, it would be much easier to become a successful theater actor, movie star, musician, writer, or director. It would be easier at least in the sense that an entire pre-established system awaits anyone interested in such professions. Nightclubs are always looking for bands, movie producers for directors, publishing companies for writers, and theaters for actors. Automatically, a guaranteed minimum number of people will be accepted to fill those roles—all one has to do is be good enough and lucky enough to be chosen. Granted, the odds aren't especially great in one's favor, but at least there are *odds*. This is not the case in the field of Independent Entertainment. No matter how talented you are, you still have to convince the guy who owns the pizza parlor—whose only source of entertainment has been a player piano with a dime slot—that a juggling act will be good for business.

"Okay. I'm Willing to Work Hard. But Where Do I Learn to Act Intelligently Silly?"

Not only are you faced with the often uncomfortable prospect of hustling up business, you are also stuck with having to learn on the job. There are no schools to teach you how best to entertain a moving line of ticket buyers or how to give a successful clown act for what seems like nine million screaming children at a backyard birthday party.

Those who desire to be musicians and actors, though, are able to take lessons almost from the time they begin to walk. Unlike them, you are forced to teach yourself.

"Gee, Maybe It's Not Worth All the Bother."

But it is! It is!

What other form of entertainment offers as much freedom? You alone, not a director or producer or agent, will decide on the material to be performed, how to perform it, the costumes, the props to be used, the bookings, the fees—everything. When you succeed, the glory and reward are all yours. Of course, when you fail...

You'll also work a lot closer with your audience than the stage actor. You can involve people directly in your show, talk with them on a personal level, shake their hands, and get to know them.

"But Have I Really Got What It Takes to Be Successful?"

That all depends on your definition of "successful." If you define it as "having a great time," then yes, you've got what it takes—desire. That gnawing hunger inside of you that wants to make people laugh and smile is the only qualification you will need to meet. All sorts of people from all sorts of backgrounds with all sorts of experience (from zero on up) have gone on to become successful Independent Entertainers. Trust the strength of your desire to give you the confidence and ability you need to learn and practice your new art. Your desire won't let you down.

"Far Out! Where Do I Begin?"

I asked myself that same question when I began my career. I didn't know the answer. There was no one to tell me where to begin. I had many books on mime, juggling, clowning, puppetry, and magic, but most of them were technique-oriented or filled with pretty but useless pictures. When they did discuss performing, the instructions were on the order of "learn these juggling patterns, get a flashy costume, and go out and give performances." Quite simply, these books were a waste of time. In fact, they were more than a waste of time. The nature in which they were written implied that all that was necessary to perform was the mastering of technical skills. Nothing could be further from the truth.

The Independent Entertainer is designed to fill the void left by technique books. It provides the information required to operate successfully, both in terms of art and business, in the unique field of Independent Entertainment. Careful use of this book will minimize any potential dangers you might face and will enable you to function efficiently and wisely as a performer.

The Independent Entertainer offers a wide variety of information that is useful to the Independent Entertainer. There are chapters on how best to learn techniques, how to perform and design an act, where to perform, and how to promote and manage your new "business." There are also chapters devoted to the unique skills (and their application) of clowning, juggling, mime, magic, and puppetry, the most popular forms of Independent Entertainment.

At the end of several chapters, I have added a very short story designed not only to be entertaining, but to point out situations, moods, and ways of thinking that an Independent Entertainer often encounters. Most of the stories contained in the book describe routines that you might use in your own act.

"What More Could I Ask For?"

You're all set. All you have to do is provide the desire (strong and sincere), the time (hundreds of hours), and the talent (at least a little bit).

But be warned! Use this book as a tool and a guide, not as a guaranteed formula. Properly used, it will save you many hours and many wasted dollars, both in purchasing or making poor equipment and in lost jobs.

I might add that even if you've decided to pursue only one field of Independent Entertainment (clowning, for example), you should study the chapters on the other fields as well as your own. There are suggestions and bits of advice that apply to all performers, which, to avoid repetition, I mention only once (usually in regard to the field to which it *most* applies). Also, I may give advice to a puppeteer that I might think no other performer would be interested in. Yet, you, on the other hand, may find that piece of information extremely valuable to your clown act. Don't cut yourself unnecessarily short.

At the very least, I hope that the information provided in this book prevents you from getting frustrated to the point of tossing your clown nose into the closet and retiring. If you were to quit, how could I possibly ever watch you perform on the corner of Seventh and Main?

Contents

Introduction   *iii*

1. Learning to Learn   *1*

2. Clowning Around   *8*

3. Puppetry   *29*

4. Mime   *45*

5. Magic   *57*

6. Juggling   *67*

7. Getting Your Act Together   *84*

8. Places to Be   *100*

9. Business Matters   *119*

10. You, Independent Entertainment, and the Rest of the World   *133*

Appendix   *142*

Index   *144*

1.
Learning
to
Learn

"HEY, C'MON, I'M A GOOD STUDENT, LET'S SKIP THIS AND GET TO THE GOOD STUFF"

I would gladly do just that, but the fact is "the good stuff" (the learning of skills) comes in so many different forms that it's a bit frightening. Do you have any idea how many dozens of magic books are in print? Or how many schools in this country teach mime? Or the number of clowns looking for apprentices? Or the possible advantages of learning to juggle by yourself?

There is no *one* way to learn anything. And each method has, as we say in the juggling business, its ups and downs. Need I point out the downs of picking up juggling jokes from books?

This chapter presents some general observations on styles of learning. In later chapters, I'll discuss in detail the specific application of these styles to various forms of Independent Entertainment.

"BUT I ALREADY HAVE A DEGREE. WHAT MORE DO I NEED?"

While it won't specifically train you to be an Independent Entertainer, formal education in any discipline of the theater arts certainly can be an asset. At the very least, it will give you the experience of being in front of people, a most important aid. It will also give you a sense of perspective and a point of reference from which to compare your endeavors in Independent Entertainment.

Remember, though, that high schools, colleges, and universities are a part of a very comfortable establishment. It stands to reason that the educational programs the establishment offers will be those that are most pleasing to the establishment. I'm not suggesting that Independent Entertainment is revolutionary, but you can bet your bottom dollar that your Theater 471 instructor would rather see you become the star of a Broadway show than doing a comedy magic act for the folks standing in line for that same show. Your instructor will try to persuade you to his or her way of thinking, both in the structure and content of classes and through personal contact.

Be aware of the influence, both subtle and blatant, exerted by the established educational system. Whether you pursue Independent Entertainment or more commercial entertainment, make sure the decision is yours.

"LET'S SEE, WHERE WAS THAT CHAPTER ON HOW TO BE CREATIVE?"

Books are fun. I enjoy them immensely. Whether they deal with the biography of a famous clown, or how to juggle, or the history of stage magic in the nineteenth century, I'll read, borrow, buy, and collect, all the books I can. Besides being entertaining, a book can be instructional. Even if it's a bad book, you can analyze the errors the author makes and learn.

Unfortunately, an instructional book is not the answer to all the problems you will face in acquiring a skill. It will not replace experience or a good instructor. A book is only a tool—handy, sometimes enjoyable, but a tool nonetheless. It is designed to do one part of a larger job, and effort, energy, and thought are needed to make it do that part.

When searching for books to be used as tools, examine each one carefully. The Independent Entertainer is often caught in the middle of two large groups of books. On one side of the shelf are hundreds of simple, colorful books geared toward children, and on the other, books that are designed for use by people involved in large commercial productions such as circuses, traveling marionette shows, and other stage productions.

CONVENTIONS

What more can you ask for in the way of inspiration than a convention of hundreds and hundreds of people involved professionally or semiprofessionally in your field? There is no other way you'll be able to see four hundred different jugglers from around the world all juggling at once, or ten thousand different puppets, or eight hundred different clown faces and costumes, or who knows how many magic tricks. A convention offers you a remarkable opportunity to study your peers closely.

Convention participants are constantly showing off their routines. After you have seen a few dozen performers, you'll begin to recognize the common approaches, both good and bad. You'll learn what works and what doesn't. You'll see the results of thousands and thousands of combined hours of practice and stage experience. You'll be able to differentiate between the confident, professional Independent Entertainer and the cocky, amateurish Independent Entertainer.

There will also be opportunities for you to perform your routine and get some feedback. A minor problem at conventions might be that the emotional energy levels are so high that people will probably love your act no matter what it consists of or how it's executed. Rational, objective criticism might be difficult to obtain.

One serious potential danger of a convention is its ability to overwhelm the novice. You might look around at the hundreds of experienced performers and think "It's gonna take me *years*, if ever, to get this good!" All I can say is, don't worry, it won't take you as long as you fear.

Even more dangerous than the self-imposed inferiority complex is the self-imposed "status quo" complex. It's easy and tempting to develop. After watching hundreds of jugglers juggle clubs all day long for seven straight days and listening to the same common style of humor all the while, it's understandable that you might begin to think, "Gee, maybe I should be telling those kinds of jokes and put more emphasis on club juggling...." Understandable, but unforgivable. That is not the independent thinking an Independent Entertainer should be practicing. The norms you see at conventions have been established because they are the easiest standards to conform to for the greatest number of people. Learn to create for yourself. Be an Independent Entertainer in every sense of the word.

APPRENTICING

If you're in a hurry to learn a skill, start hunting for an experienced Independent Entertainer. Become his apprentice. There is no faster way to acquire knowledge and skills than from a private tutor.

If you personally don't know anyone under whom you might apprentice, keep your eyes and ears open and eventually you'll run across a puppeteer or clown doing local work. Find out when he's performing and see the show. If you like what you see, talk to him. Tell him how great you thought his act was and explain that you'd like to learn to be as talented as he. There's a good chance at this point he'll ask you to apprentice under him. If not, don't be shy—ask him.

The established Independent Entertainer is frequently in dire need of an extra hand. He needs someone to help him set up and tear down quickly, someone to move props into the right places at the right times, and maybe even someone with whom to perform.

The advantages for you in this sort of relationship are tremendous. While your tutor shoulders the responsibility for the show (contracts it, creates it, directs it, provides props and transportation), all you do is reap benefits. You will learn all sorts of little tricks unique to Independent Entertainment, tricks that may have taken your tutor years to learn. In ten performances, you will learn what it took him a hundred performances to learn. In addition to the tricks, skills, and other useful knowledge you will acquire, you'll gain experience and confidence, items that come slow and hard when working by yourself as a beginner.

Working as an apprentice does not mean you are a partner. Don't expect to be paid much, if at all. Don't expect to share in decision making. And don't expect to share in the glory of applause. You will not be allowed to be the star of the show. Take orders, do what you're told to do, and *learn*.

Be careful not to mold yourself into the image of your tutor. Just because Walter the Wild Magician says a certain trick is done best in a certain style, that doesn't mean that style is best for you and your execution of the trick. Maintain your independent thinking, and don't blindly follow a leader.

LEARNING ALL BY YOUR LONESOME

Teaching yourself—no school, no tutor, nothing but you—is the most difficult approach to learning and, you guessed it, the most rewarding. For the Independent Entertainer, it is the most obvious approach.

You'll pay your dues. You'll make mistakes and feel like a fool. You'll have audiences ignore you. You'll get stuck doing shows where neither you nor anyone else has any business doing one. You'll learn the meaning of trial and error. Fortunately, the rewards are well worth the price you'll have to pay.

Your show will stand a good chance of being unique and original. In a world of thousands of jugglers, clowns, mimes, and puppeteers all doing pretty much the same nondescript acts, you'll earn a special sort of pride and confidence. You will be truly independent.

EXPERIENCE

You've heard it before, I know, but it's true: Experience is the best teacher. Nothing in the world can do for you what the experience of performing your first few shows will do. Nothing. The point is, don't waste too much time on conventions, schools, books, building fancy props, or all the rest. Get out there in front of audiences and *perform!*

Ah, I can hear you now. "I've only been juggling a few months and I'm still working on all these neat tricks that I *need* to be able to do if I'm going to give a good show." I say, do the show without the neat tricks, even if it won't be as good—even if it's a bad show. If people see how you do your magic trick, or if they don't understand that you are trying to blow up an invisible balloon, or that your puppet talks without moving his mouth, don't worry about it (but don't ignore it, either). You will learn more in your first few shows than you imagined there was to learn. You'll learn what people enjoy and what they don't—a good clue as to which direction your future practice and emphasis should take.

There is nothing to wait for. Hurry up and begin performing!

For those reading this book who've done considerable amounts of performing, I remind you that a good performer never stops learning from his experiences. Too often I've seen performers who have put together a tight, successful act and quit listening to the audience's reactions and examining their own performances. The day a performer feels that he doesn't need to listen to his audience or that his act is beyond improvement is the day he starts going downhill.

A WARNING ABOUT WARNINGS

Unfortunately, there will be many people, relatives included, who will try to convince you that not only are your attempts at becoming an Independent Entertainer ridiculous, impossible, insane, and foolish, but that even should you chance to succeed, the effort will be greater than the reward. While these people mean well, you must learn to ignore them. If you have to, tell them to mind their own business.

You must maintain, as I suppose all artists must, a sense of blind confidence in your ability to succeed. You have no time for negative, pessimistic thoughts. Absolutely *no* time. You will succeed. It's simply a matter of patience and determination.

Now, anyone for learning the tricks of the trade of clowning?

2.
Clowning
Around

PASSING THROUGH CLOWNTOWN....

The most commonly pursued form of Independent Entertainment is clowning. While this is due in part to the myth that clowning is easily learned, the most important factor in its popularity is its potential to earn money. There are always jobs available for the clown—many more than there are for other Independent Entertainers.

In addition to the commercial benefits of clowning, it has been my experience that at least a minimum of clowning experience helps tremendously in developing performance confidence in other fields. If you happen to be interested in performing magic or any other non-clowning field, I strongly urge you to make the additional effort and learn some clowning. Consider it a learning experience, a paying of dues. It won't be a waste of your time. You'll find yourself opening up and performing bizarre and outlandish antics, thus making it easier for you to operate more comfortably in your non-clowning act.

It is financially wise to have clowning down to a practicable skill. If you can't swing any jobs with your puppet act, it's nice to fall back on an always needed clown show. There may very well be other forms of Independent Entertainment you'd rather be practicing, but if clowning helps put food on the table, it can't be all that bad.

For those interested in being nothing but clowns, welcome to happy times. You're entering an age-old, respected profession. It is filled with a rich and colorful history. It's fun. In terms of costumes and props, it may require more energy than other forms of Independent Entertainment, but in terms of talent, it requires only the enhancement and exaggeration of your own good-natured self.

THE FACE! THE FACE! LOOK AT THAT FACE!

When you walk into the room, the first thing anyone will see is your face. Your audience will quickly pass a verdict on your character by the evidence of your face alone. They'll decide if you're really a nice guy or just another phony out to make a quick buck. If your clown face doesn't match your actions and style, they'll perceive a discomforting disparity and be less willing to accept you. If they like your face, you're well on your way toward having your audience in the palm of your hand.

Don't consider your face to be a mask. It isn't a layer of goop you can hide behind. Consider your clown face a modifier of your natural face. A clown face is always most effective when it enhances your own everyday happy-go-lucky character.

It'll take you a while to find a face that's right for you. Many clowns go for years searching for that "perfect look." When they find it, many actually go through the process of getting it patented. More than one case of face-lifting has gone to court.

When you do find the right face, you'll know it. You may experiment with many different styles, but there will always be one face you'll find yourself coming back to. That's the one you want to keep.

Towel and Bar of Soap Before you apply anything to your face, clean it. Always start with a clean, oil-free base. If you've got them, shave those whiskers close. Nothing feels or looks as weird as makeup applied over a stout stubble.

Mirror At first, you'll be able to put your clown face on in front of your own bathroom mirror. Eventually, though, you're going to have to do the job in the field. Buy yourself a small mirror. A pretty handy size is a 6" x 6" mirror, although you might like to have something larger. On occasion, I've been forced to use a purse-sized compact mirror, with acceptable results. Whether or not you want to invest in a professional cosmetic mirror with soft lights all the way around is up to you. It's rather lavish for the Independent Entertainer.

Nylon Stocking, Cap, or Bandana Any one of these items will serve to hold your hair away from your ears and face. The application of makeup then becomes much simpler, quicker, and

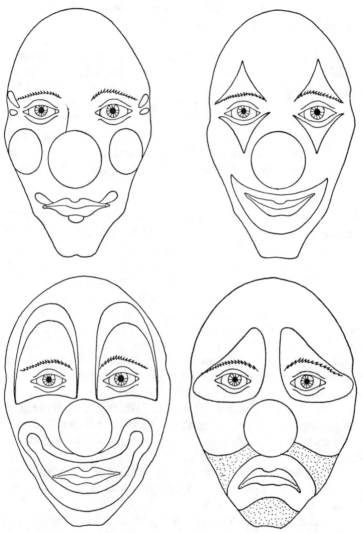

Figs. 1-4 Clown faces, from simple to complex to sad; easy to apply with ample room for modification

neater. I've found that the nylon stocking works best. It's light, tight, and takes up very little storage space.

Towel You'll need one or two towels that you won't mind throwing away eventually. These will be used for wiping off excess grease paint from fingers, ears, and sinks. It's nice to have a soft towel for the final portion of cleaning your face, which will be a bit raw at the end of a day.

The best size for towels is washrag size. If they're much bigger, the used portions will dangle and drag across your shirt as you clean your face. A small towel also requires less space in storage.

White Face Here we go. You're either looking at a tube or small can, wondering if you really want to smear that goop all over your nose and lips and eyelids. *Of course you do!*

Get a nice-sized blob on your fingertip and start with your cheeks. For the moment, don't go much below the jawline. Work in toward your nose and chin, making certain to cover all of your face, including the lips. Move back toward the edge of your ears, then to your temples, and across your forehead. Be careful around your eyes. Cover your eyebrows with white face, but not your lashes—it might get into your eyes and cause irritation. (When applying makeup around the eyes, remember that the heat from your body could cause it to melt and run into your eyes.)

There, now your face is white. Take that one finger that applied the white face (you didn't go and get two fingers dirty, did you?) and smooth out the lumps and heavy spots, making everything uniform.

The neck, if it's not covered with a big collar, will need some white face, too. Apply it more lightly than you did on your face. Blend it in smoothly at the jawline.

Always put white face over your entire face, even if you know you'll be putting red grease paint on your nose, blue squares over your eyes, and red stars on your cheeks. Colors have an annoying tendency to stain skin if you haven't applied a base layer of white face.

Baby Powder Baby powder, when applied to the face, absorbs excess moisture, keeps the shiny, greasy look down to a minimum, and somehow works to keep the white face bonded together.

Buy a container of powder, and dump it into a thin, tightly knit sock. No holes, please, and tie a good, strong knot at the end. You now have a perfect powder applicating tool. Slap it gently against your face, and the powder will seep through the material and stick to the white face. Store your sock in a plastic bag.

What to do with the extra sock? Carry your marbles in it.

Grease Paint Grease paint comes in a short, stubby, crayonlike shape, wrapped in foil. There are at least two dozen different colors available, but you won't need that many. The only colors I've ever used are red, yellow, blue, and purple.

Directly apply the stick of grease paint to your face. Do not use your fingers. Apply it carefully, because where the grease paint goes, it stays. Covering mistakes is a terribly messy operation. The best thing to do is to clean off everything (white face included) and start over.

I suggest that you always start applying grease paint around your eyes. After the eyes are completed, paint your mouth. Now move on to all the little extras, like stars on the cheeks and polka dots on the chin. You'll find it's easier to match the extras with your eyes than your eyes with the extras.

While there are an infinite number of ways to design a clown face, there are a few practical guidelines to follow. First, work toward a face that enhances your own natural characteristics. Your face has lines and contours that can be developed to create a very attractive image. Don't work against yourself by trying to create a face that *isn't there*. Study your features carefully and work with them. Second, be careful not to look bizarre. I once did a show looking like a member of the Kiss rock band and all the little kids began crying in fright. One way to avoid looking bizarre is to use as little red as possible, especially around the eyes.

The third general guideline to follow is to develop a face that can be applied quickly. I pity the clown who spends two hours before every show carefully applying his detailed face. I have my time down to five minutes. It isn't necessary for the Independent Entertainer to have a complex, elaborate face. Those that do have such faces tend to be either overly proud of their artistic skills or insecure about their character as a clown (the old "hide behind the mask" complex). An elaborate face is not only a great consumer of valuable time, but it has nothing at all to do with the actual performance.

Eyeliner The eyeliner pencil is used for outlining all the grease paint. It can also be used to outline the entire face around the hairline and the lower jawline. It serves wonders in providing clarity and definition to shapes. Have you ever had a problem in balancing the colored areas on each side of your face? You'll find that all your problems are quickly solved with an eyeliner pencil. An extra heavy outline on one side can make your face look bigger or smaller. After you've applied grease paint and liner, repowder your face.

The Nose The first thing children will see is your nose. It is the shining crown jewel on a sea of grease paint, white face, and baby powder. They will scream with delight at its size, point at it, or trick you to bend over so they can rip it off. Well-mannered children will get down on their knees and beg for the mere privilege of touching it with a fingertip. Your nose is a never-ending source of joy for children.

When you are first starting out, you can get by with applying some red grease paint to the lower portion of your nose. Eventually, though, you will come to realize that red grease paint is only second-rate to a big chunk of bulbous rubber.

I bought my clown nose for a dollar and a half. It's round, has two tiny nostril holes, and is made of a soft rubber that is held in place by means of an elastic string that goes around my head. Every now and then, I'll get a comment on the string, but not often enough to change anything. Most kids don't even notice the string. It makes the clown nose easy to put on or take off, and you don't have to worry about it coming loose.

Some people use rubber cement to keep their clown nose in place. This can be a real drag. If it doesn't fall off on its own, it is likely that someone will rip it off, and then where are you? You can't perform without a nose, and you often can't take the needed ten minutes to reset it, either.

If you prefer, you can make your own clown nose from a Ping-Pong ball. Cut a hole in the ball so that it will fit comfortably and securely over your nose. Cushion the edges with cloth tape. Paint it a nice shiny red (the *only* color for a nose), and put small holes in each side of the ball for the elastic string to fit through. Nostrils are optional.

Your clown face is now complete. White face, grease paint, eyeliner, powder, and nose. You're ready to roll.

What's that? You have an itch beneath your eye? And you're afraid to scratch it because it will smear that beautiful little purple star to smithereens? I can certainly sympathize with you. Try poking directly on the itch with your fingernail without smearing anything. Push hard—even pain can be a relief from that maddening, greasy itch.

Roll of Toilet Paper The show is over, you're back home, and the makeup is beginning to drive you crazy. Time to clean up. I begin with toilet paper, using one square at a time. It's compact and less expensive than tissue paper. Wipe it firmly over your face to remove as much paint as possible. Grease paint, especially red, that has seeped through the white face will be more difficult to remove.

Cold Cream Buy a very large jar of cold cream. You'll soon use it all and will save a few pennies an ounce by buying the largest size.

Apply the cold cream to either your entire face or to small portions at a time. Work it in thoroughly with the remaining makeup. Doesn't that feel nice? Now wipe it off with a few more squares of toilet paper. A final cleansing with soap and warm water will finish the job. If your face feels a bit raw from the makeup and rubbing, apply some skin lotion.

The Container Keep all your cosmetic material, including towels and mirror, in one separate container. Any small bag or box will do fine. For a long time, I managed with a cardboard shoebox. Use the smallest size container possible. There's no need to carry around empty space and extra weight.

THE THREADS

Now that your face is taken care of, you're going to have to get dressed properly. You won't be able to find the proper clothing overnight. You'll have to search through many a Salvation Army Store and garage sale to find what you need. What you can't find, you'll have to make.

Save yourself grief by starting out simple and cheap. It's better to work your way up to more detailed and expensive clothing than to start out that way and discover you prefer the ragamuffin hobo look. Besides being less expensive, secondhand clothing seems to present a more approachable image to an audience than fancier, flashier, custom-made clothing.

Starting from the top....

The Hat Almost any style of hat or cap will work. Make sure it will stay firmly in place when you bend over or take a prat fall. Do not use a hat of such high quality and cost that your heart will break if an egg is broken on it or if a rambunctious child throws his pizza at it. If your hat looks too plain and dull, sew on a few blue and pink patches, or stick a plastic flower in it.

While I've always used a soft denim cap, it would be nice to have a stiffer hat for flipping about and easily catching things in.

Keep your costs down to a minimum. Zero is a good figure to aim for. There are too many hats hanging around in the closets of this world for you to spend good money on a new one.

The Wig Unless your natural hair is so terribly unsightly that not even a bright hat won't perk it up, avoid using a wig. Not only are they hot and uncomfortable, they don't look right on an Independent Entertainer. Fluorescent green or orange, the standard clown wig colors, are just bizarre enough to make young children leery of you when up close. For the circus clown who needs colors that shout out to a distant audience, it's another matter.

White Gloves You don't need them. Some clowns feel that every inch of their natural body should be covered and insist on wearing them. Some circuses require all their clowns to wear them.

Gloves will make you feel warm and will limit the agility of your hands. They will get stained and will not look so white. They can be difficult to locate in stores and might be very expensive. They completely mask the one part of your body that can come into physical contact with your audience. Nobody enjoys shaking a gloved hand. A glove defeats the purpose of that form of contact. The feel of flesh touching flesh can be very comforting to the child who is trying to figure out if you're a nice person or just another cartoon image that might explode or run through a wall.

Shirt Your shirt can be a pullover or button-up, short sleeve or long (most clowns prefer long). As long as it's expendable, looks like fun, and feels comfortable, it will work. If you don't own anything very colorful, sew on some bright patches and stick a bandana in a pocket. Better yet, stick in a flower of the water-squirting variety.

Pants The bigger and baggier the pants, the better. If the pants are in too good a condition to look like clown pants, rip off the cuffs so they look scraggly and too short. Sew on some patches. Also, the bigger the pockets, the more goodies you can carry inside.

I've had great success with a pair of everyday overalls. Not only do they have several huge pockets, along with many tiny ones, they are easy to slip into. They can also be worn for other functions, like grocery shopping.

Suspenders If you don't use overalls, you'll surely need a set of suspenders. Not only do they hold your pants up, but you can stick your thumbs under them and s-t-r-r-r-e-t-c-h! and then let them snap back against your chest and knock you over. You can also display all the buttons you'll collect in your career in a neat little line for everyone to see.

Jacket A carefully chosen jacket will add distinction to your attire. Will it be a snazzy blue and orange smoking jacket with pink patches on the elbows? Perhaps the happy-go-lucky hobo look? A tuxedo with balloons tied to the tails? I've seen them all in secondhand stores for under a dollar.

Socks Socks are simple. Yours can be knee-high and vibrant, wild and crazy. Never wear a matching pair. Children find it uproariously funny when your socks are different colors. One yellow sock plus one blue sock equals big laughs.

Shoes This is the only area of clothing where you should plan on investing a chunk of bucks. Yellow or red tennis shoes will pass for the part-time clown, as will a large pair of rickety looking boots. But for the serious clown, only a size 35 will suffice. When wearing large clown shoes, you will hear members of your audience whispering, "Say, look at those shoes! He must be a *real* clown!" And when children jump up and down on them, you won't feel the least bit of pain.

Where can you get professional clown shoes? The last time I checked the clown and circus newsletters, the going rate was $75. "Yikes!" is right. Lucky for you, I can tell you how to beat that price, or maybe even get them for free.

Take an old pair of brogans to your local cobbler and have a large pair of clown shoes made out of them. The cobbler will know what to do. If you are both friendly, you shouldn't have to pay more than $30 or $40 for the clown shoes. If you're willing and the cobbler needs some promotion, offer to walk around town on your stilts and proclaim the virtues of his or her establishment. It's a fair trade for a pair of shoes.

No matter how you get them, *get them!* The money you

spend on shoes will come back to you many times over in the extra bookings they'll bring. Large clown shoes will distinguish you as a professional.

Bow Tie Buy one that is very big and very bright. Attach it with a band of elastic so you can stretch it out and snap it back.

The One-Piece Jumpsuit Clown Suit This is the easy way out. It's neat, orderly, and handy. Just stick your arms and legs in, zip up the back, and that's that. A jumpsuit can be very attractive and perfectly fit people's conception of what a clown should look like. In dire moments, when a performance is due on short notice, a jumpsuit is handy to grab and jump into.

Though the jumpsuit is convenient and acceptable, I advise against wearing one. It's too easily used (and frequently perceived) as a mask. It is not as much an extension of one's own unique character as a carefully chosen wardrobe of common clothing can be. I have found that the masking of a character—with jumpsuits, fluorescent wigs, gloves, and elaborate faces—removes the challenging prospect of being genuine, personal, and entertaining. In addition, I have frequently noticed that the performance quality of masked clowns is below par. However, this is not intended as a blanket criticism. I know one clown who wears a one-piece suit, a wig, and gloves, and has a very detailed face, yet she is the warmest, kindest, most sincere clown you would ever want to meet. I make these comments only to help you think about everything you do and wear. The more you think and analyze, the more you'll enjoy what you do and the better your act will be.

Costume Container I always roll up my clothes in a linen sack. Others use a small suitcase. Either way, you'll need a container for your clown clothes. When a job comes up on short notice and you are pressed for time, you want every article of clothing to be available immediately so you don't have to run around crazily looking for everything. And none of this searching for a jacket that your friend thought was so funky he "just had to wear it to the movies last week and now who knows where it is?" business. Your clothes are professional tools and not to be loaned.

WHAT'S A CLOWN WITHOUT HIS PROPS?

What kinds of props are you going to use? Does the Rube Goldberg side of your mentality shine brightly when devising gadgets whose operation makes eyes pop open wide? Do you have Charlie Chaplin's ability to make any simple item at hand into a prop and pull dozens of laughs out of it? Whichever prop work you choose to use, remember that both styles require your own unique intelligence and skill in order for you to perform successfully. Good props alone do not make a good show.

COLLECTING AND BUILDING

While you are excited to begin collecting and building the many props you'll need, remember that it is going to be a long and tedious task. You can avoid great amounts of frustration by knowing there is no way you can do it quickly.

The most expedient route in obtaining props is to collect the ones that are ready to go and need no major alterations. Collect everything you can get your hands on: golf clubs, baseball bat, tennis racket, hot water pad, plastic dishes, pillows, rope, string, yo-yo, sunglasses, ladder, horn, squeaking rubber duck, fishing pole, chair, mop, cap gun, squirt gun, big clunky camera, bowling ball, rubber snake and/or chicken, to name but a few items. These are easily collected when cleaning out the average American garage.

The props that you build usually serve a unique function in an unexpected manner. Props that are guaranteed to get kids jumping out of their seats buzz, squirt water, beep, smoke, boom, explode, and disperse confetti over large areas.

All of your props will work better after they've been treated with coats of several different colors of fluorescent paint. What could be better than a bowling ball with glowing pink polka dots? It may be tacky, but it's loads of fun.

Your skill in using props and creating skits will develop gradually. You need to remember only two variations in developing humor from props. First, use the prop in an obviously improper manner. preferably in one that appears to inflict pain on your body. Second, have the prop function in an unexpected manner.

YOUR TOY BOX

You won't have built or collected too many props before you see the need of a practical storage box. This box should be able to fit in the back of your car. An added luxury to the box is a set of wheels for easy transportation from the car to the area of the performance. A necessity is a latch and lock to prevent kids from emptying it when your back is turned.

WHERE DO THE $$$$$ GO?

Strive to keep your expenditures down to a minimum. If your eyes are kept open and your fingers sticky, your only costs should be for items like tape, paint, and glue. If you are careless, you can easily spend hundreds of dollars on props and costumes. Try not to be in a hurry to obtain any one item, for this is when you are most likely to pay top dollar. Collect props as they come your way, even if you don't have an immediate use for them.

JOKES

Memorize a collection of jokes to use both between skits and during the entire routine. If you can't think of your own, go to the children's section of the library and check out an armload of joke and riddle books. Memorize a list of elephant jokes, puns, bad news and good news jokes, and what-you-get-when-you-cross-a-this-with-a-that jokes. Have the jokes on the tip of your tongue so you can fire them out right and left.

Also, have quick replies to throw back to the wise kid who shouts out "You're not a real clown! You're just a man with makeup on his face!" (I've heard that exact line more than once.) Have a line ready that will relieve the tension and discomfort when a little toddler breaks out in screams upon seeing you. You can be very spooky to toddlers.

Most of your jokes will come ad lib as particular situations arise. Occasionally, I've heard myself tell a joke (actually, it was the clown who said it, not *me*) that was so funny that I stopped and laughed at it myself—very unprofessional, I'm sure. It's a secure feeling to walk into a show without having anything too definite planned, knowing that you will be able to improvise a funny, successful performance. There's a little secret to good ad libbing, though—one that many clowns fail to explore and develop. It's called involvement.

THE JOYS OF INVOLVEMENT

Kids have the most fun when they feel involved in the act. Unlike adults, they haven't learned to be lazy. They want to do something!

I've found it's best to keep audience involvement centered around the group as a whole, rather than around individuals (for example, using several volunteers for tricks, and so on). Kids feel comfortable acting in a group and will reinforce and encourage each other. The children's involvement also makes it easy for you to focus the energy of the entire audience on yourself. Let them provide the noise, excitement, and enthusiasm while you sit back and direct.

GIVING AWAY GOODIES

A form of individual involvement that works without any major snags is the handing out of goodies: funny pictures, candy, balloons, coupons, or any one of a number of other fun items. This is best done as an ice breaker at the beginning of a show, as a way to get things rolling. Kids also enjoy having things to look at and show to their friends as evidence of having seen and talked to a real clown.

Animal balloons are without doubt the best giveaway item. I'm not talking about the round, helium-filled balloons, but the long skinny ones for which you need iron lungs and strong lips to blow up (or even better, a professional iron balloon pump priced right at $10). You'll only need to inflate a few of these before you're able to make an entire menagerie. Your anxious admirers will be understandably patient as you sculpt each work of art. While making giraffes and hippopotami, you'll have time to talk and make jokes with individuals, giving them personal attention. Some clown acts consist of nothing but balloon work!

Unfortunately, giving away candy can be potentially dangerous. For some strange reason, children show no signs of proper upbringing when it comes to the prospect of receiving free candy. Their eyes begin to glow, and their arms and grasping fingers reach up, blindly, relentlessly....

BEING CAREFUL

You are not a full-fledged clown until you have paid the dues of being mobbed, kicked in the shins, slugged in the back, tripped, stripped, and used as a target. Rambunctious eight- and nine-year-old children (especially boys) are the main offenders. My good friend Toby T. Twist the Clown says these children see a clown as a cartoon figure who can run through walls, explode, be flattened by steamrollers, run over by trains, dropped from airplanes, and always bounce right back into shape. Parents say the kids are having a good time and releasing energy. I say, be careful.

When possible, the best way to deal with a problem is quickly to walk away into an area where the meany will hold back. If you can't do that, try to sidetrack the child. If even that fails, move *fast* and grab the youngster firmly by the collar or shoulder (but don't cause injury). Drop the clown act. Speak to the point and be dead serious. Make it clear that he or she had better knock it off or there'll be big trouble. The shock of such a sudden change in your character should be enough to hold the child in line. If not, tie the troublemaker to a chair.

LEARNING TO ACT INTELLIGENTLY SILLY

If as an apprentice you can latch on to an experienced clown, you've got it made. Should that option not be available to you, check out the alternative education programs in your area for classes in clowning. If neither option is available, you're going to have to plug away determinedly on your own. Fortunately, audiences are very receptive to the beginning clown.

In your first few shows, don't try to act as silly and crazy as you look and feel. Be reserved. It's common for beginners to be so self-conscious and nervous that they move too fast and talk too loud. The audience will be able to see right through this; children will be frightened by and unable to follow the fast movements, and adults will feel uncomfortable with your nervousness. Take it easy. Don't worry that you are ignorant of experience and the knowledge that goes along with it. It's a fact that you are working to change, and there's nothing more you can do about it. The only time to worry is when you no longer learn from experience.

Your own unique style will gradually develop. Of course, it doesn't happen by accident. It requires hard work, careful attention, and long hours. Maintain your enthusiasm, and learning will be a joy.

WHAT'S IN A NAME?

Whatever name you decide on, stick with it. Don't mess around with a growing reputation by asking people to keep up with name changes. And be careful not to use another clown's name. I recently heard a story of a clown who sued his own son for using the same clown name the father had been using during his entire career. Like faces, established names are private property and patentable.

I think there might be a growing tendency for clowns to use their own names as stage names. I know a Debbie the Clown, a Bob the Clown, and myself, Happy Jack the Clown (I can't help it; that's my name on my birth certificate). Perhaps the trend toward using real names is part of an effort to reduce the masking of a clown. Besides, no matter what you call yourself, kids are always going to call you Mr. Clown.

WHY IS IT FUN TO WATCH A CLOWN? HOW MANY STARS ARE IN THE SKY?

Many an academic paper has been written on the clown as a figure of pathos who represents the foibles and tragedies of everyman in such a manner that we must laugh to prevent tears of pity and sorrow. This sort of speculation is all well and good for the frustrated poet turned clown, but for the Independent Entertainer juggling rubber chickens at the grand opening of a carpet store, it offers little.

I could present to you all sorts of discursive theories on why a clown is entertaining, but the very best answer comes from children and their parents. It is so simple that at first one might doubt its validity. The answer is found in the laughter itself (hmm, *Zen and the Art of Clowning*). Clowns are fun *because they are fun*. After you've performed a few dozen shows and talked to children and their parents, you'll begin to see the truth in this reasoning.

A SIMPLE ROUTINE FOLLOWED BY A SIMPLE GESTURE

1

It was Kristy's fifth birthday party in as many years. It was Mr. Clown's forty-fifth birthday party in less than one year. He was beginning to wonder if he really was cut out for this sort of work. He could always go back to school and get his degree in Industrial En— "Hey, can I tell the kids you're ready to come out?" Kristy's father poked his head into the kitchen from the back porch. "They're beginning to wonder if you're ever going to perform."

"Be right there." Mr. Clown snuffed out his cigarette and picked up his bag of many colorful tricks. For forty bucks, I guess I can't keep 'em waiting too long, he thought.

2.

Everyone had been having a wonderful time with Mr. Clown's Super Special Show. Everyone except Billy. Billy cried when Mr. Clown wouldn't let him touch his big red nose, even though he let everybody else touch it. "My nose is tired" was all Mr. Clown said. And there was Timmy, who got slapped lightly when he tried to look into Mr. Clown's bag of tricks. Timmy sulked for a while, but like Billy was now having a lot of fun.

Mr. Clown looked at his watch for the umpteenth time. "Okay, kids, time for my very last and very best trick in all the world, but first I gotta find my balloon. Have any of you guys seen it?"

The children screamed in unison, "It's right there, Mr. Clown, it's right there!"

Mr. Clown seemed impervious to the fact that a balloon floated behind him. It was tied by a string to his back belt loop.

"Aw, c'mon," said Mr. Clown, you guys are kidding me. I don't see any balloon."

"No, really, it's right there behind you," squealed Kristy. She pointed frantically, "It's right there! Turn around!"

Mr. Clown turned around and looked and looked, but didn't see any balloon.

"Nah, I don't see any balloon behind me. You guys are playing a trick on me."

Kristy stood on her chair and waved her arms.

"But it's right there, Mr. Clown! Look behind you but only don't move and you'll see it!"

Mr. Clown was glad that these children weren't over sixty—if they were, the frustrating excitement of the balloon hunt might give them heart attacks.

"Okay, I'll look behind me but I won't turn around." Nobody noticed that he pulled the slipknot from the balloon string when he turned around. "I don't see anything. You were fooling me about that balloon."

"Look! It's up in the sky, Mr. Clown, it's floating away! Hurry and look!"

"I'm not gonna fall for any more of your tricks. I'm too smart for that. Hey! Look what I found!" He pulled a balloon out from his sock. "The biggest balloon in the whole world. Why, this balloon is bigger than my whole garage! I brought it just special for this birthday party. What should I do with it?"

"Blow it up! Blow it up!"

Mr. Clown tilted his head back, put the balloon on his lips, and blew it up into the air.

"No! Not like that! Hold onto it!"

So Mr. Clown held it in his fingers and blew at it. "Like that?"

"No, put it in between your lips!"

"Oh, like this." Finally he did it right. "Do you think this balloon is big enough?" After only one puff of air, they didn't, "If you want me to make it bigger, tell me 'bigger'" "Bigger!" "What's that? I can't hear you." "*BIGGER!*" Another puff, another "Bigger!" The tension grew faster than the balloon. Finally, a carefully concealed thumbtack ended the show with a bang. It was 1:30. If he hurried, he could catch the last quarter of the football game on TV.

"Bye-bye, kids. Time for Mr. Clown to go away."

Kristy ran up to him, still squealing and smiling. "What about your other tricks Timmy said you had?"

"I don't have any more tricks. Bye-bye, everybody!"

3.

"Here's your money. You know, you clowns charge more than plumbers."

"Makeup's expensive these days."

"Yeah."

4.

After throwing his bag of tricks into the back seat, Mr. Clown turned around and saw a familiar little girl standing on the sidewalk. "Who are you? Is your name Sam?" he asked. He smiled and dug his keys out of his pocket.

"No, I'm Kristy."

"Hello, Kristy. Bye-bye, Kristy."

"You were just at my birthday party, Mr. Clown."

Oh yeah, yeah, yeah, jeez, thought Mr. Clown. How could I forget she—

"Mr. Clown?"

"Yes?" And make it short, birthday girl, I've got a game to catch.

She ran up to him and wrapped her little arms around his big leg in a giant hug. She squeezed her soft, curly head against him. "I love you, Mr. Clown." And then she ran back to her birthday party. Mr. Clown stood speechless.

5.

Kristy's father opened the front door.

"What's up? Didn't give you enough money?"

"No, sir, it's not that. I just happened to find a few more tricks in my trunk and I thought the kids might like to see them."

Kristy's father smiled. "Hey, they'd love that."

Let's hope so thought Mr. Clown.

3.
Puppetry

Puppetry is an ancient form of theater, dating at least as far back as Ancient Greece. Throughout history, it has been practiced primarily by the Independent Entertainer. Some puppeteers who became too satirical to suit a reigning government are known to have lost their heads.

It has only been recently that puppetry has undergone a tremendous change that could prove beneficial to the Independent Entertainer. Thanks to Jim Henson and his Muppets, puppets have moved into the top echelons of commercial entertainment. The Muppets compete successfully with TV detective shows, disco musicals, and Robert Redford movies. While you knew all along that puppets could please mass audiences, the rest of the world didn't. Henson and his Muppets have significantly expanded the audience for the Independent Entertainer.

HOW A SHY, BASHFUL ARTIST WHO HIDES BEHIND CURTAINS CAN STILL BE A SUCCESSFUL ENTERTAINER

Puppetry is unique in that it is the one form of Independent Entertainment in which your body is not necessarily seen by the audience. Many people who would never dream of performing in front of other people have thrived and flowered while hiding behind the curtain of a puppet stage.

Puppetry also has a special appeal to those who are talented in various forms of visual arts. I know of two women in New Mexico whose wonderful work in sculpturing was eventually applied to the creation of ceramic puppets. They enjoyed being able to give voice and movement to their creations. Many other artists have turned to puppetry for this same reason.

The skills of puppetry are easily learned (with the exception of marionettes). Find an interesting voice that fits the puppet's character, practice operating the puppet for a few moments, memorize your lines, and you're ready to give a show. There's really not much more to it than that. So what are you waiting for, huh?

TYPES OF PUPPETS

The three most common types of puppets are rod, marionette, and hand puppets. For the very Independent Entertainer who is concerned with transportation, ease of production, money, and time expenditure, there is only one puppet to consider—the hand puppet. For the not so Independent Entertainer who enjoys creating complex puppets and elaborate shows and who isn't worried about being efficient and economical in his use of time and money, there are the more demanding options of rod puppets or marionettes.

Marionettes Marionettes are dolls with hinged joints operated by overhead strings. A marionette may have as many as sixteen different string-controlled functions. Operating such a mechanism while delivering lines is a skill that cannot be learned overnight. And if you think operating a marionette sounds like a nightmare, try making one. Construction of these puppets is an art in itself. I strongly advise against attempting such a project unless you have professional supervision, are very handy at constructing small, delicate functions, and have plenty of free time. Harsh advice, I know. But if only someone had warned me.

Marionettes are used primarily in large commercial stage productions. I am referring to the productions that travel state fair or school assembly circuits, or that reside in a permanent marionette theater. Large productions tend to use marionettes for two reasons. First, they are larger than hand puppets and are more easily visible to larger audiences. Second, there is a strong sentiment among people who are "into" puppets that marionettes are the cream of the crop, the ultimate puppet, perhaps because marionettes take so much time to construct and to learn to operate that their use is a sure sign of one's dedication to the art. Many of these people seem to have lost sight of the essence of entertainment and have become enamored with the beauty of elaborate contraptionism.

Personally, I don't like marionettes. Let's face it, they look downright weird. While they are strictly and obviously mechanical

Fig. 5 Marionette   Fig. 6 Rod puppet

in design, they bounce and float eerily across the stage floor, thus creating a disturbing dichotomy of appearance and action. Their faces are eternally frozen in one expression, the only possible movement being the zombie-like lowering and raising of the bottom jaw or the rolling of the eyes. No way to ignore it, marionettes can't help but look strung out.

Rod Puppets Rod puppets are a sort of upside down marionette. The operator holds a rod which is connected to the inside of the puppet from underneath. On this rod are strings and levers which operate the puppet's many functions.

A rod puppet offers a distinct advantages over its mechanical counterpart, the marionette. The rod puppet operator can maneuver more easily than his marionette counterpart. The solid grasp on the rod allows the puppeteer to move the puppet quickly and precisely. This produces a more pleasing and natural movement, at least to my eye, compared to that of marionettes.

Like marionettes, though, rod puppets are challenging to build. And the audience still knows they are mechanical devices because of their rigid functions. And have I mentioned broken strings? Or strings that get tangled in the middle of soliloquys? Perhaps I'd better knot.

Hand Puppets A hand puppet fits the needs of the Independent Entertainer like a glove fits the hand—perfectly.

Where should I begin to discuss the innumerable virtues of the hand puppet in regard to the Independent Entertainer? Noticing the thinness of your pocketbook, perhaps we'll start with the cost.

If you have a few rudimentary sewing skills and a few scraps of material on hand, your puppets will cost you nothing. If you can't sew and are unable to dig up any friends who can, you can go to your local toy store or drugstore and buy a nice puppet for anywhere from three to ten dollars. The cost of hand puppets, both in time and dollars, is far below that of marionettes and rod puppets.

The storage of hand puppets, unlike that of the fragile mechanical sort of puppet, is no problem. I have treated my hand puppets rudely, occasionally shoving them into my juggling case between a bowling ball and an extra pair of shoes, and those little guys are still in one piece and smiling.

The size of a hand puppet is just right for the Independent Entertainer. Most of your work will be for small audiences of no more than a few dozen people. They will all be able to see your puppets perfectly. For what it's worth, I've even successfully executed routines for audiences of up to one thousand people with my little hand puppets.

The nicest thing about hand puppets is that they allow for an incredible amount of warmth, creativity, and expression. It is not a mechanical device to be operated by strings and levers. It is an extension of your own flesh and blood. It is wrapped snugly around your hand and wrist, with your fingers operating—no, not operating, *being*—the mouth and face. All expression and movement of the puppet comes directly from your body, with no intermediary element to distort or minimize the message your mind wishes to communicate. The audience sees a smooth, naturally moving puppet that functions as though it were an organic entity. The audience also sees a face that can express an almost infinite number of emotions.

Like a properly designed clown face, a hand puppet allows for the expression of the puppeteer's own emotions. Your audiences, while they may not be fully aware of this in their minds, will sense and admire your genuineness.

Remember, too, that you are an Independent Entertainer. Your audiences are usually small, informal, and friendly. Doesn't it make more sense to use the intimate hand puppet than the pretentious, mechanical marionette or rod puppet?

CURB YOUR ENTHUSIASM!

Before delving into production techniques, let's consider the direction in which you want to go. Are you going to work just a few

Fig. 7 Hand puppet

Fig. 8 An inexpensive, thoroughly believable stage

puppets and use no other props? Are you going to work with a very simple, functional stage? Or, like most overenthusiastic beginners, are you going to go for the "big production"?

It's easier for puppeteers than other Independent Entertainers to get wrapped up with the idea of the big production. You start thinking, it would be nice to have a curtain to work behind, maybe a velvet curtain, and stage lights, maybe lights with gels and dimmer controls, and gee, with a nice set-up like that, I ought to produce *Snow White and the Seven Dwarfs*. That means I'll need another three operators, and maybe someone to work the lights, and if I have that many people I'll need a bigger stage. Maybe I should rent the school auditorium, sell tickets, print posters....

Do you see what happens? While these are all good, interesting, challenging, and rewarding ideas, they involve a great deal of time, energy, and money to accomplish. Do not attempt the big production until you have acquired some solid experience with the simpler forms of puppetry. Otherwise, it will be a frustrating, exhausting experience that is likely to end in both financial and artistic failure. Even nationally renowned puppeteers with large shows are frequently operating on the brink of financial disaster. If you are an Independent Entertainer who is concerned about being financially responsible, don't kid yourself into thinking that you can start right off the bat with a big production. Start at the bottom.

THE STAGE

The whole world's a stage, so why build an extra one? Especially if puppets are a part of another act—say, clowning or mime—there's no need for one. With my puppetry (short skits with two puppets), I've never used one. Audiences seem to have no problem accepting my face and body right behind the two puppets I hold. In fact, I think audiences like to see me. The presence of my body makes the existence of the puppet more honest and more real than if I were to hide behind a stage.

This is not to say that all puppet performances should have the puppeteer in view. Children's shows, especially full-length plays,

Fig. 9 Traditional, flat, limited, boxlike stage

are best performed on a stage. A stage allows for the smooth exit and entry of different characters and provides a formalized area toward which children can direct their attention.

It's up to you and your needs when deciding whether or not to use a stage. I suggest that as an Independent Entertainer you should try to do without one whenever possible. You are not bound by the constraints of tradition.

LITTLE PEOPLE

In terms of potential earnings, your best bet is to gear your act toward children. That's where the money is.

Traditional titles are going to have the most appeal and bring in more bookings and larger audiences. Parents will forever be taking their children to see *Cinderella* and other staples of children's literature. Your own production of *Ralph and the Non-Electric Clock*, though no doubt a literary *tour de force*, will have potential customers thinking twice.

Write all of your own material. Don't use published plays. Besides the matter of paying royalties (you *were* going to do that, weren't you?), a published play just isn't as much fun to produce as your own creation. You can use traditional titles and respective plot lines and themes, but add your own dialogue and color.

One long play is not always feasible to perform for the Independent Entertainer. Sometimes you'll be working under conditions where you'll be able only to perform short skits. Many puppeteers do whole shows comprised of nothing but short skits. A series of short skits also makes it easier to maintain high energy levels and audience attention.

As you gain experience and commercial success in puppetry, you'll want to develop a repertoire. One way to guide its growth is to produce seasonally attractive plays. At Christmas, perform *The Nutcracker*. At Thanksgiving, do something on the order of *The Mouse on the Mayflower*. Once you've produced a play, you'll have the script, puppets, and whatever other props you've made, ready to use again whenever needed.

BIG PEOPLE

If performing for children just isn't where you're at, regardless of the money potential, there's no reason you can't turn your puppets loose on adults. Satire, comedy, and drama are all viable options. Such options offer challenging material to the puppeteer, and they can also be made challenging for the audience. Old ideas can be expressed in this refreshingly unique medium. Hopefully, this will cause the audience to examine these ideas with a fresh approach and a renewed interest. There's a good chance this will happen. Look at it this way: If puppeteers have had their heads guillotined for their political skits, there must be strength in puppetry's ability to communicate. Let's hope, though, we never see the Sesame Street Seven on trial for subversive activities.

YOUR VOICE OF MANY COLORS

Finding the right voice for your puppet takes time. Talk to it—er, him. Ask him about his life history, where he grew up, women he's loved, mountains he's climbed, and his plans for the future. If you run out of subjects, there's always weather, religion, and politics. Slowly but surely he'll come out of his shell and tell you all about himself and reveal his true character. He'll become more comfortable and relaxed, losing the strain in his voice. After he tires of talking to you, introduce him to one of your human friends. Let the two talk for a while. Your puppet needs to meet other people and learn how to conduct himself.

TESTING, ONE TWO THREEERRRRRRRRBIZZZZZZZZ....

If business is going well and getting better, consider investing in an amplification system. There are times when you'll be performing that your natural voice will not be able to carry over extraneous noises. This is often the case in busy pizza parlors and other inherently noisy locations. Also, if you operate from behind a curtain, your voice will be muffled. Since the dialogue is usually essential to a puppet routine, you'll need an amplification system to guarantee that the audience can hear you.

You won't need a big, expensive system for the small areas and crowds you'll usually be performing for. Many home stereos are capable of amplifying a microphone input. While these work fine, you might find that in the long run you would be better off with a very small, inexpensive, professional amplification system. These are rugged, dependable, and not too expensive.

Tie the microphone around your neck instead of mounting it to a stand. Since you need to move and bend over and turn around while talking, you can't be glued to a fixed microphone.

While an amplification system is an added piece of mechanical equipment, it will allow you to give performances in more situations than before. Be careful, though, not to use an amplification system when it isn't necessary. All too often I've seen performers use microphones for small, quiet audiences when their own naturally amplified voice would have worked fine. Audiences in these situations can't help but feel a bit offended and disturbed by the use of unnecessary machinery for an intrinsically simple, pure form of entertainment.

THE BIG DECISION: TO RECORD OR NOT TO RECORD?

A pre-recorded soundtrack (to a full-length theater production) can be a valuable asset. You can do ten shows a day without worrying about your voice giving out; you won't have to rely on other performers/operators to memorize and give quality delivery of lines; and you can add music and sound effects and see to it that each line is delivered precisely the way you want it delivered.

On the other hand....

A soundtrack locks you into a frozen pace with no opportunity to experiment with new lines or deliveries. Your creativity during a performance is effectively reduced to zero. In terms of authenticity and energy, the pre-recorded soundtrack cannot compete with a live delivery. You aren't selling an audience your skills as a performer, you are selling them a viewing of a production.

While it is to be avoided whenever possible, there are times when the soundtrack is a virtual necessity. When you have more than one puppet operator (what if your assistant gets sick and you have to use someone who doesn't know the lines?) or when you are doing a half dozen or more shows a day (and begin to lose your enthusiasm), you'll find that the advantages of a soundtrack outweigh its disadvantages. It's at least a good idea to have one ready for emergencies.

Producing a soundtrack can also be a very challenging and creative process. A good soundtrack is something to be proud of. The proper voices for each role will have been chosen carefully. You will have direct control over deliveries and pacing. Music and sound effects will give a touch of class and professionalism to your production, helping to fill in the "empty" periods in a play and adding to the warmth that is lacking without your natural voice.

RECORDING

For recording and editing purposes, make use of a four-channel tape recorder. You can record two tracks of dialogue: one of music and one of sound effects. Each track should be recorded separately. Avoid using a tape recorder with sound-on-sound capabilities. Such a system will allow you to add music and sound effects to the dialogue, but at great risk. They will be added to the same track that already contains your dialogue. There is no erasing. Suppose your music is too loud or starts at the wrong time?

Prior to the recording of dialogue, make sure you've had a chance to work privately with each actor. He or she should know exactly what you want before entering the recording room.

When your actors are assembled, get them to begin working as soon as possible. It's easy for them to waste a lot of time joking around and telling stories. Save the fun for after the recording. This is business for you. You will be using this dialogue in your show for years and years, so concentrate and get the most out of it. After a few rehearsals, turn the recorder on. Make at least two complete recordings of the script. If an actor blows a line or doesn't deliver it quite the way you want it delivered, don't worry; ask him or her to repeat it. You can edit out the mistakes later.

Wonders can be worked with editing. I once made a twenty-minute film using seven different puppets and voices. Unable to get the actors together in one spot at one time, I recorded each of their voices separately. When I had recorded all of the dialogue, I edited it together in its proper sequence. It sounded perfect. However, it had taken more than seven times the work that would have been necessary if I'd been able to get everyone together in one group.

Choose the best recording and transfer it to a cassette tape for performance work. Cassette players are small and easily carried, unlike reel-to-reel players.

Take good care of your master copies. You will slowly develop a repertoire of plays that can be performed easily, even on a moment's notice. Eight years from now, you can pull out your master copy from your archives, transfer it to a cassette, and perform. Make sure, though, you've memorized your play. If the tape gets tangled or the batteries run low, you could be in a lot of trouble.

LEARNING ABOUT THE BIG PRODUCTION

The Independent Entertainer can learn puppetry as it applies to his needs without instruction, only practice and determination. Learning about big productions is another matter. You can forge ahead and learn the hard way (frustration, failure, and loss of money), or you can work for a short while in someone else's production.

Big productions are always looking for volunteer labor to operate puppets; do voices; make puppets, backdrops, and props; sweep the floors; and sell tickets. There's a remote chance you might even be paid for your efforts. In New York, unemployed actors are sent out by their labor union to temporary employment in puppet theaters.

Very possibly, you'll find yourself working with someone who is doing his first production. Watch him closely and learn from both his mistakes and smart moves.

Be dependable. Help yourself and your employer by being a hard worker who is always available when needed. You will establish yourself as a good guy in the local puppeteer community and develop a habit that will be beneficial to your own private work. The usual volunteers in the puppet productions disappear shortly after the novelty wears off and the hard work begins.

"I HEAR YA, I HEAR YA!"

Tom the Nod, the almost cute puppet, profusely thanked everyone at the end of the show. Still, not a coin was dropped in the cup at the base of the makeshift bamboo and taffeta stage. This would be the last church rummage sale to see the Tom the Nod Show.

One young man came forward. Tom the Nod looked back and forth between the cup and the young man. The young man pulled out some of his long hair that had blown into his mouth and spoke. "I just wanted to say, man, like, I think your whole gig is really out, you know, and like, it's an inspiration to me. You're beautiful. Truly." He spoke slowly and with a random pattern of intonation.

"Gosh golly gee, that's heavy," Tom the Nod said in his usual raspy squeak, not sounding the least bit sarcastic. "What grand actions have I unknowingly set in motion?"

"Huh? I don't catch your drift, man."

Tom the Nod sighed. His voice might have lowered an octave. "How have I inspired you?"

Recognition struck. "Oh, yeah! I do some mime and juggling, you know, and like, seeing your act around town and stuff, well, it's shown me that it's what I wanna do full-time, you know. I'm gonna travel around the world performing." He cocked his head and peered into the distance. "Yeah. That's what I'm gonna do. It's my path."

Tom the Nod's mouth fell open. Then his body fell sideways and hit the stage. "Cozzzzmic."

"Fer sure it is, fer sure. Well, hey, it's been real, man, but uh, I gotta be moving to another time/place. Keep the peace." He started to turn. Tom the Nod turned him back.

"What?" screamed the almost cute puppet. He bent forward and peered mercilessly into the widened eyes of the young man. "What?"

The young man was mildly surprised. "Oh, hey, I sense a discordance in you, man. You'll find a macrobiotic diet will really help you tune in with— "

"I am perfectly in tune, thank you. It's my pocketbook that isn't."

"Ah. Materialism was never my thing. I always— "

"Let me rephrase that, oh brother. This guy wants some cold cash in return for what you've enjoyed, learned, and derived. Listen, fella, take a look in my cup." The fella listened and looked and then wowed real mellow-like. "You got it, Jack. Not one thin dime. And that's from seven shows. And now you. A compatriot in the arts. A (sheesh!) brother, so to speak. One whom I've inspired to pursue a noble line of work. Exactly how *do* you expect to eat when *you* travel the world and perform?"

Tom the Nod looked right through the young man's eyes and into his heart. Right through his heart and into his pockets.

"Smiles are cheap and easy. Only a transfer of material commodities, preferably crisp and green, will tell you how much people value your gifts. Coins in the cup tell you the *sincerity* of appreciation."

The young man considered this new line of thought carefully. "Hmm. Yeah. I hear ya, man, I hear ya." He dug into his pockets. "Here's eight cents, it's all I got." Tom the Nod said nothing. "Alright, and here's the last of my food stamps."

"Thank you, kind sir. Consider it a very inexpensive education you have received here today. Good day. And good luck in your travels."

The puppeteer put the last of his equipment in the trunk of his Caddie, hoping desperately he had gotten the idea across to that thickhead. He tossed his measly earnings into a bag marked "Charity" and drove to his office to catch up on some work. He was thankful that puppetry was only a hobby, and not his means of support.

4.
Mime

What other form of Independent Entertainment offers as many advantages as mime? You don't need any props and only a small pocketful of makeup. You don't need to be heard. You don't need any special stage arrangements. Not having to accumulate props, along with being able to learn easily and quickly, you can begin performing mime sooner than any other form of Independent Entertainment.

Ouch! You dedicated mime artists don't need to scream so loud! All I said was that mime is easily learned. Yes, I understand that you've been working at it for years and continue to have lots to learn. But it is still relatively simple for the Independent Entertainer to master mime to the extent that he can perform an entertaining, enjoyable show. A few weeks' practice may not prepare one for a show at the Kennedy Center in Washington, D.C., but it will prepare one to perform sidewalk shows at the Main Street Shopping Center.

LEARNING

The best option to pursue is to enroll in a mime course. Mime courses are generally offered by the theater department of most colleges and universities, by adult education programs, or by alternative education programs. If you live an a large city or college town, a mime course is surely available to you.

You can learn quickly and with confidence in a mime course, especially if you practice with devout dedication. The more you practice, the more your instructor will be able and willing to help you. Learning in a class is even better than learning in a tutor/apprentice arrangement. You will not only have the trained, professional guidance of an instructor, there will be a dozen or more other students for you to examine. Learn from them. Find out what they're doing wrong and how they go about trying to correct it. Watch for any unique little quirks they might practice and see if you can use them in your act.

Sharing a learning experience with others can be a lot of fun, too. You might make some good friends in the class, and maybe even perform with some of them on a professional level. Learning with other beginners also helps to conquer any qualms or uncertainties you might have about performing in public. It will definitely help you feel more relaxed at your first few shows.

If classes or private tutors aren't available to you, your learning will be slowed but in no way stopped. Apply yourself. Get hold of a large mirror and study your face and body. Whoever the first mime was, he had to teach himself, didn't he? There's no reason you can't do the same. With all the mime performances you've seen live and on film and television, you already have a solid idea of where you're headed and what you want to accomplish. That's more than the first mime had going for him.

As with all other forms of Independent Entertainment, experience is the best teacher. When you are able to go through ten to fifteen minutes of material without forgetting anything, take your act to the streets and shopping centers and perform. It's alright, really. No one is paying you, so whatever you do is fine. Audience reaction will tell you right away which movements are discernible and which aren't.

SKILLS TO PRACTICE

Warm-up Exercises Start your practice session with a few minutes of vigorous stretching and waving. Move every part of your body: arms, legs, head, neck, torso, and even nostrils.

Remember that your body is a tool to be used in communicating specific messages. The more control you have over your body, the more specific the message will be. You will find that breaking down body movements to their smallest units enables you to exercise the most control.

Before going any further, grab a paper and pencil. You are going to make an inventory checklist of your body movements. Start with your toes. Curl them down, curl them up, start with your little toe and move in to the big, start with your big toe and move out to the little, move only your big toe, and so on. Continue this process with each part of your body all the way up to the top of

Fig. 10 A mime in basic costume and face, pulling an imaginary rope—its entire body is working to define and operate an object

your head. Always remember to strive for the smallest, most singular movement. Move no other part of your body but that which you decide to move.

Body Operations These are all the practical, identifiable, non-abstract motions that your body performs in real life. They include no other object than your body. Common operations include walking, running, swimming, skipping, dancing, and so on.

Be efficient with your body in performing these operations. Remember that your body is a tool used in communicating. Excess movement interferes with the message, while sloppy movement muddles the message.

Particularly keep an eye on the beginning and ending of each movement. Make these parts distinctive. Give them clarity. Put a *snap* into them.

Defining Objects Defining objects is done by touching them, lifting them, poking your finger into them, showing how slippery they are, or how heavy and how hot they are. Practice defining ten or twenty objects, and call a few friends over. Have them watch and see how many objects they can identify correctly.

Operating Objects You'll find this easier than defining objects. Push a broom, swing an ax, bounce a ball, eat an ice cream cone, type a letter, and—Hey! Watch it! I just saw you moving too fast and letting your motions slur into one sloppy blur. Clean up your act. (Practice taking a shower.)

Emotions In learning to properly express emotions, you are going to have a tendency to rely too heavily on your face. You are also going to over-emote, both with your face and with your body. Remember what I mentioned about efficiency. The swallowing of one good-sized lump will do more to show your audience that you are scared than all the shaking and quivering in the world.

Learn how to use your body (minus face) to express emotions. Again, ask a friend or two to identify the emotions—only this time perform for them while wearing a bag over your head. You'll be surprised at how resourceful you can be. This little exercise will reduce significantly your dependence on your face. I am not saying it is wrong to use your face, only that you should learn to incorporate the entire body in communicating emotions and that you should not rely too heavily on the face.

MATERIAL

You may be the most technically skilled mime in the world, but without the proper material you'll leave your audience wondering and wandering. With good, interesting stories and sketches, even a beginner will be able to entertain an audience and bring a bit of magic into people's lives.

If you have trouble creating your own material or are timid about testing it out during your first few performances, there is a good deal of proven material available that is commonly used by many mimes. Make use of it. Contact a high school or university theater instructor, and ask for mime material.

Using abstract and avante-garde material may be intellectually challenging and satisfying to you and your peers but not to the bulk of audiences you'll be performing for as a commercially successful Independent Entertainer. If you decide to use some of the material, use it carefully. Your audience is probably watching you because they want to have fun, not because they want to get heavy.

INVOLVEMENT

When doing informal, up-close work, it's nice to get your audience in on the act. Hand items to them: a balloon to hold, a cat to pet, three balls to juggle. They'll love to participate in your imaginary world.

Unless they appear particularly gifted and willing, avoid having the audience do too much creative work. They can become nervous and freeze (which will embarrass you as much as the victims). And if they happen to be *too* creative, there may be no stopping them.

Another option to pursue is to take requests for improvisational subjects. That'll keep you on your toes. Yet another option, recommended only for very informal events, is a form of involuntary involvement. Mimic every motion and gesture of a particular spectator. This takes a talented mime to perform successfully. Be careful not to do it for so long that you annoy your victim. You may not be able to mimic his strong right cross.

THE THREADS

You'll want to wear physically unobtrusive clothing that is simple and interesting, yet not visually distracting. A leotard or tight pullover shirt and loose, colored or black pants are pretty much the order of the day. Ballet shoes or simple thongs are fine for the feet. If you prefer, you can work barefoot.

THE FACE

The mime wears a face to hide his personality. He wants the audience to focus only on his motions, not his non-mime, everyday character as shown by his natural face. With the use of white face and simple lines, the mime creates a face that is not connected to the person wearing it. It is not the face of a particular human being, it is the essence of every human face. The mime can mold his face into any character he wishes.

The ultimate extension of this thinking is to use masks. While the theory behind using masks—(complete removal of the individual's personality from the stage—may be sound, it tends to create a bigger problem than it solves. The mask is so obvious, so blatant a concealment, that it draws a negative attention from the audience that interferes with your performance. White face, on the other hand, inconspicuously blurs the individuals personality. The audience doesn't even realize they are supposed to be missing something.

If you do use a mask in any part of your act, use it for a specific purpose—not as something to hide behind. Use it to create something your face can't accomplish on its own. A mask in the style used in Greek theater lends itself admirably to sketches of tragedy and pathos. Masks in the style of the Mummenschanz Players (rolls of toilet paper for eyes and mouth, for example) will impart a great deal of fun and novelty. Masks in the style of your own choosing will impart_____(you fill in the blank).

Back to the white face. You'll need everything the clown needs in the way of cosmetics. You may decide you can do without the grease paints and rely solely on the black eyeliner pencil. I find that it's nice to have the option of having red lips or blue nose now and then. You'll need to exercise more care in applying a mime face than a clown face. You're only going to have a few lines (accent of

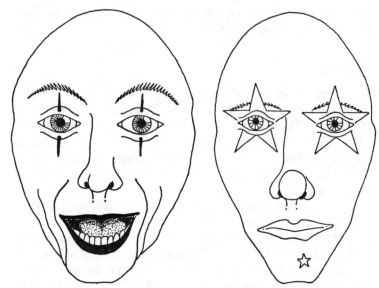

Fig. 11 Traditional mime face

Fig. 12 The more imaginative star-struck variety

the lips, horizontal and vertical lines through the eyes, and an outline around the entire face) to work with, and you want them to be perfect. Don't paint a smile on your face. Make your lines neutral so that they may be used for whatever emotion you wish. Your makeup should modify the essence of the human face.

PROPS

For the mime who is an Independent Entertainer, props can be more of a disadvantage than an advantage. You have to collect them. Spend money on them. Store them. Carry them. Keep an eye on them. Worry about them breaking. Depend on them.

Are they worth it? Right now, you can walk out of your home in costume with nothing in your hands, ready to perform. Can you carry all your props on a bicycle? On the subway?

The props that you do collect should be in their simplest form, conveying only the essence of what they happen to be. If you decide to use a walking cane in a routine, don't use a fancy one wrought with curlicues when a simple stick will suffice.

TITLE CARDS

Many mimes write the titles of their different routines on large pieces of cardboard or paper. These are presented to the audience prior to each respective routine. These cards can serve a valuable function in directing the audience in what to see and look for. Title cards will help eliminate hushed questions: "Is he swinging an ax? Working on a railroad? Swatting big flies?"

THE OLD STARVING ARTIST ROUTINE

1.
The Growl

—Gggrrrjjjzzzzblip— "I sure hope they can't hear that." *That* was Robin's empty stomach. *They* were the dozen or so people who happened to be eating in the ice cream parlor at the time of Robin's surprise mime and storytelling performance. It was an unscheduled performance—Robin had made a very quick deal. One show in exchange for all he could eat. His usual charge was twenty or twenty-five dollars, but the economy had been slow this winter, and he was very, *very* hungry.

On with the show, thought Robin. The sooner I finish, the sooner I eat.

2.
The Story

"Tonight, ladies and gentlemen and children, I will present to you the story of a magician from the days of long, long ago. A magician who performed only in exchange for warm fuzzies. He never ever—despite great temptation—worked for those yikky green slimies. He would always perform on street corners and in little taverns and parlors, not too different from this wonderful establishment, in fact—and always for warm fuzzies. And do you know how he began his act? Why, with his famous magical juggling act, that's how!"

At least this juggling act will keep their eyes up in the air and off of what's left of my shoes. Wish there was a free rapid transit system in this town, Robin thinks.

3.

The Act

The mime pretends to juggle three balls. He tosses some behind his back, under his leg, off the floor and off his head, amazing himself to no end. He juggles three balls with one hand. No sweat. He takes them back into his hands and throws one ball very high—and it doesn't come back. He jumps up and finally grabs it in both hands. His hands are wrapped around and completely conceal the ball. Suddenly, his eyes go wide. His hands began to jump around. Something alive is in his hands! Hmmm. He peeks in. *Ouch!* He got poked in the eye. The object in his hands suddenly takes on a new energy and pulls him all over the room, smashing him into walls, over chairs, through the kitchen area, and back again. The mime finally regains control and is angry. He decides to squeeze the object to smithereens. At the very last second, his curiousity gets the better of him, and he decides to take one more peek. Hello! What's this? And to think he was going to squeeze it! He unfolds his hands to reveal a fluttering butterfly (his hands are crossed and flapping). The butterfly slowly flies out and away from the mime, leaving him to wave goodbye.

Wish I could fly away, too, thinks Robin, to someplace warm and dry where I didn't have to worry about heating bills every time I turned on the furnace.

4.

The Rationalization

"And that was the magician's first trick, turning a ball into a butterfly. He did that trick everywhere he went, for anyone who cared to watch. There was no other magician in the world who could do that trick, or even any of the many other wonderful tricks he performed. He was the very best there was.

"But was he a wealty man? No, no, indeed not. He wouldn't accept cold slimies in exchange for his work. And we all know what cold slimies are, don't we? Cold slimies are the things that buy golden trinkets and large, lavish homes, servants to polish your toenails, and luxurious clothing and goodtime friends, etc., etc., ad nauseum. Not that this magician would have minded having a few of those items—not at all, not at all. In fact, there were many opportunities to have such wealth. Big entertainment tycoons offered him the chance to earn more cold slimies than he could ever dream of spending. But then he would have had to work on a big stage with his audience way far away, not close up like I am with you. And he'd have to wear the clothes they told him to wear, and do the tricks they told him to do, and worst of all—only the rich people could afford to see him perform in theaters.

"This magician would have nothing to do with that sort of arrangement. He would continue working for warm fuzzies and warm fuzzies alone! Warm fuzzies, decided the magician, were the best thing of all, better even than gold and professional toenail polishers. Warm fuzzies—say, you all know what warm fuzzies are, don't you? They're kinda like—hmm. The closest thing to warm fuzzies that we have today are big smiles, hugs, hearty laughs, clapping and cheering, handshakes, and kisses on the cheek. Or the feeling you get when you make someone extra happy. Warm fuzzies. That's all the magician wanted.

"Now, another trick this magician did was the Great Bompswog Turnaround Trick that..."

Gggrrrrjjjzzzz—Please stomach, just another fifteen minutes and we'll be eating.

5.

The Envelope

"Here you go, three ham sandwiches. That right?" asked the cook.

"For starters," answered Robin. His mouth watered.

The cook handed him an envelope. "Here, some guy left this for you."

Robin sat down and swallowed two sandwiches before opening the envelope.

Robin, very nice act. Excellent. In appreciation I'd like to offer you this cold slimy, otherwise known as a hundred dollar bill. Suggest you reconsider your firm stand on cold slimies and big tycoons and contact Rog Iverson at New Age Concerts. He needs some opening acts. He'll be expecting you. Use this money. Warm fuzzies are neat, but don't go far in shoe stores.

Robin looked around the room with his mouth open. No one. Ggggrrrrjjjjzzzzz...

**5.
Magic**

I have some good news for you. There is money to be made in this business. Did you ever hear of Isaac Fawkes? He was a street magician who worked in eighteenth-century England. He had what could be called a very successful business. In fact, he died before he could spend his last ten thousand sterling pounds. Would that all street performers could suffer the same plight!

Okay, maybe he was an exception. But there are still lots of things going in your favor. No other form of Independent Entertainment has exclusive nightclubs in which to perform. And most every town in this country has a magic shop. No other form of Independent Entertainment gets as much television coverage, either. These factors indicate that there is a fairly large and stable market to which you can sell your skills.

It also means you're likely to have some competition. Magic, along with juggling, has a great following of practitioners who do it as a hobby. These people will frequently do shows for "fun." Why would anybody ask you to perform for money when they can get someone else to perform for fun? That is an interesting question that has stymied and frustrated many an Independent Entertainer. Fortunately for you, I have an answer.

You'll be hired to perform because you are unique. In a world cluttered with nondescript, look-alike magic acts that haven't changed in fifty years, yours will be like a breath of fresh air. Don't worry about competing with the hundreds of other magicians on their level. Create your own standards, and there will be no competition.

LEARNING THE TRICKS OF THE TRADE

Plan on learning magic by yourself with the aid of instructional books and purchased tricks.

You'll find more magic tricks in books than you'll ever be able to use. You shouldn't have any problem finding at least a dozen instructional books in any bookstore or library. Don't disregard the books for children. While many of the tricks in these books are simple, they can still be entertaining.

The only advice I can offer you on learning a trick is to keep practicing, even after you think you have it mastered. Be able to talk and think about other things while doing the trick. Be able to do it with your eyes closed. The operation of a trick must be second nature to you. If it isn't, keep practicing.

PROFESSIONAL HELP? HEH, HEH, HEH!

Getting professional help is almost impossible. Oh, you'll get an occasional bit of advice, maybe even a trick or two, but no training of any substance. As successful as a magician might be, he is always in competition with a large number of others. He can't afford to spend time training young upstarts who will soon be chasing the same dollars he is.

Most professional magicians have no need for a partner. They may have a female "assistant," but you can be sure she's a wife or daughter or close friend of the magician. (More on Sexism in Independent Entertainment in Chapter 10).

THE ACT

While the particular tricks you perform are important, they are not the sole factors in determining your success. Perhaps even more important than the tricks is the manner in which you present yourself on stage. Avoid placing too much emphasis on the tricks—alone they are only tools to be used in entertaining an audience.

SAY, WHAT'S THAT BIG BLACK THING UP IN THE SKY?

Misdirection is a skill that is frequently abused by beginners. It is the emphasis of an action that is unimportant to the execution of the trick, committed to distract attention from whatever sneaky thing you are doing.

An unskilled magician will commit a single act of misdirection: a cough, a quick turn of the head, or the delivery of the punch line of a joke. This single action has the unwanted effect of telling the audience you're pulling the string. They may not know *how* you tricked them, but they'll know when you did it. The aura is shattered.

Successful misdirection is not the single, simultaneous cover-up action. It is the development of a *constant line* of misdirection. The misdirection is subtle, entertaining, and evenly paced. That's the big reason the execution of your tricks should be second nature—it frees your energies to work on misdirection.

SAY, WOULD YOU MIND DOING THAT TRICK AGAIN?

Yes, you would mind, thank you!

Never repeat a trick. Never. Frequently, the beginner will do this when working in front of children. They'll beg you to do tricks over and over again. It's tempting to do, too, because their begging shows that the children are having a lot of fun with you and you would like to keep it that way. But resist the temptation.

Succumbing to their desires not only has the effect of putting them in charge of the show, but you run a good risk of having them figure out your trick. Many times some clever little wit has correctly blurted out my secret in an accusing tone of voice.

SECRETS ARE SECRET

Never reveal the secret of a trick. Not even to your girlfriend or best friend, no matter how much they plead with you. I speak from sad and embarrassing experience. I once had a friend who was on the verge of insanity trying to figure out the secret of the "linking rings." He was losing weight, getting jittery, the works. What else could I do? I told him the secret. As the words rolled out of my mouth, I knew that what I was doing was more cruel than letting him waste away. A look of utter shock and horror spread over his face. He seemed repulsed by my very presence in the room. "Is that all?" he asked. I felt as if I had just told a four-year-old child that Santa Claus doesn't exist.

Audiences don't want to know how you do your tricks. They think they do, but deep down they enjoy the mystery more than they would the knowledge.

Should one or two members of your audience, either during a show or afterward, tell you how you did a trick, don't give the slightest indication of whether the guess is right or wrong. As positive as people might sound, they're still not so sure that they would bet their life on it.

Never tell anyone anything about your magic. Constant vigilance is required by you and all other magicians to maintain the state of the art, so mind your p's and q's.

TUXEDO, ANYONE?

Standard costume for the magician has been the tuxedo. There is nothing wrong with the tux. Audiences certainly seem to have no problem accepting it again and again, year in and year out. Still, wearing a tux makes you look like every other magician every member of your audience has ever seen. You may or may not find this to be a disadvantage to you and your act.

The only time the Independent Entertainer may find a distinct advantage in wearing a tux is when doing shows for older, very conservative audiences. Wearing a tux will make you look like the magicians in Las Vegas and on television specials, which is top of the line as far as audiences are concerned. *Hey, they'll think you're SUPER!*

WORKING WITH ANIMALS

Unless you are willing and able to give your animals (rabbits and doves, mostly) the care and attention they deserve, along with always being able to guarantee their safety at performances, please don't use them. Even if you do have the time to care for them, it would be wise to avoid becoming involved with the extra responsibility.

CATEGORICALLY SPEAKING...

I find it easy to divide magic tricks into two distinct categories: sleight of hand and gimmicks. Sleight-of-hand magic is solely the function of your dexterity. It is the manipulation of objects that makes the trick, not the hidden device within. It is often referred to as "close up" magic, since it can be done (if you're good enough) right under a spectator's nose. It is a respected magician who can perform good sleight-of-hand magic.

There are thousands of gimmicky magic tricks on the market or described in books. While they take less skill to operate than sleight-of-hand tricks, people enjoy watching their operation and trying to figure out how they function. I use only two gimmick tricks: linking rings and the disappearing ball. I use these because of their simple, basic eye-pleasing shapes, and because their gimmick is relatively simple and still requires a great deal of dexterity. Many gimmick tricks require all the dexterity of pushing a buttom.

I admit to a certain bias against performing gimmick tricks. I enjoy watching them, though. I mention this only because I have run into several other Independent Magicians who have expressed the same feelings. Precisely why this attitude exists, I don't know. Perhaps it stems from a dislike of relying too heavily on mechanical devices as the main point of interest in a trick, not the performer's skills in entertaining and dexterity.

MAKING TRICKS

Building your own tricks will not only give you a sense of accomplishment and pride, but you'll know your tricks look like no others in the world. You might even save a few dollars in the process. You can either duplicate tricks whose operation you know, or you can devise your own. Each trick will require a good deal of time and energy to build, but it might well be worth the effort in the long run. Too many magicians purchase every single one of their tricks from mail-order houses and stores. This is what helps establish a typecast "look" to magic shows.

BUT THEN AGAIN....

Now that I've denegrated the concept of purchasing tricks, let me tell you how wonderful they can be. With a very small investment, you can set yourself up with all the fancy looking tricks you'll need for a show. Why waste time building them?

While other magicians may own the same trick, it doesn't mean that your performance will be identical, or that audiences don't want to see a repeat of a trick they've seen performed before. Look at how many women you've seen sawed in half on television. That trick is one of many perennial audience favorites. (By the way, the last price I saw quoted for that trick was $1,300. Saws included.)

STORAGE

Make sure your storage container has a lock on it. After and before shows, everyone will want to get their grabby little hands on your goodies. The only way to politely stop those hands is with a lock. Don't mess around.

The size and number of props you use will determine the size of your storage container. Some professionals need semi-trucks to haul their equipment. The Independent Entertainer will wisely try to make do with one or maybe two suitcases worth of equipment.

THE SHOW MUST GO ON

1.

David and Dennis, the eleven-year-old twins of Ellis Street, took the last 25¢ admission fee from one of their friends.

"Everyone grab a seat," shouted David. This was supposed to be funny, as the only seat in the garage was the floor. "The great magic show begins in a few moments."

"I don't see why we couldn't have waited another week or so to do this show," whispered Dennis to David. "We still don't know these tricks very well."

"We need the practice," answered David in the same hushed whisper. "I talked to Mr. Harding, and next week we get to do the assembly show at middle school."

"What?! There's no way we're ready to— "

"I know we're not ready, but if we're gonna be famous, we gotta get started fast. This is only small-time stuff, anyway."

2.
Bam!!

Dennis and David both jumped. All the kids looked back at the door and became silent. Big Lee. He'd slammed the garage door against the wall. Big Lee was big. Bigger at least than the kids he picked on.

"Hey, Lee, comin' to the show?" Dennis asked, trying to sound brave.

"What does it look like, fatso?" Lee answered. Dennis resented that. He didn't think he was as much fat as he was a little too chubby. David felt the same about his own body.

David shook the money box and jangled the coins. "Everybody is supposed to pay a quarter, Lee." There was a pause and everyone waited.

"You're lucky I ain't chargin' you to let me see this dorky show." Big Lee snapped his fingers at John, Timmy, and Kurt (his favorite victims) and told them he wanted their spot. "Let's get on with the show, man. The Double Bubble Magic Show, isn't that right?" Big Lee laughed at his joke.

"What are we gonna do now, David?" Dennis was again whispering. "This guy's gonna mess up everything."

"One always has to deal with the unexpected in this business." David answered. Just don't blow the tricks and keep the show moving."

3.
Dennis and David were in the middle of their third trick—the disappearing quarter trick. Up to this point, the only trouble Big Lee

had given them was to yawn real loud and snicker and boo. David though Dennis had been doing pretty well under the pressure.

Suddenly, Big Lee faked a kick at Dennis. Dennis jumped and dropped the quarter, which rolled right into Big Lee's hand. He pocketed it and said, "Now that's a real good disappearing act, you double doughboys—audience participation and all. I like it. I truly like it."

John, Timmy, and Kurt started to get up to leave. If there was any more trouble, they sure didn't want to be around when it happened.

"Everybody wait a minute!" shouted David. "Nobody should leave before they see the great trick that Larry Houdini was famous for." This eased the tension and the boys sat down again.

"It was Henry Houdini," corrected Dennis.

"Whoever. He went by many names. Now we will need a volunteer from the audience—someone strong and intelligent. John, how about you?" David's eye was on Big Lee.

"John nothin'. I'm gonna do it." Big Lee popped up, and no one was about to argue. "You dopes haven't done a trick yet that I haven't seen through."

Before he knew it, Big Lee was blindfolded and handcuffed. "Better not try anything funny, man, or you've had it."

"Nothing funny at all, Lee," David said confidently. "This is serious business. Now just lean back into the box—there—okay, now! Help me, Dennis!" Dennis still wasn't sure what they were doing, or why, but in a few seconds they had Big Lee locked up in the large luggage box they used for storing their tricks.

David shouted to Lee in the box. "The trick is to escape, Lee. I'm sure that as strong and as smart as you are, you'll figure it out in no time. We'll be waiting for you."

Muffled shouts of anger were all they could hear coming from inside the box.

"Timmy and John, take this box outside. We'll let him out after we've finished the show. Maybe later this evening."

Timmy and John, along with all the other audience members, giggled as they dragged the box out of the garage. Beneath the giggles, Dennis asked David what in the world he thought he was doing?

"If we're gonna be famous magicians, we can't let anything or anyone get in our way. The show MUST go on, all the time, every time."

"Yeah, but Big Lee—"

"See how everyone is smiling?"

"Yeah, but—"

"It's okay, I understand. The first show is always supposed to be the hardest show."

"Yeah, but—"

"After we do the assembly show, I'm gonna ask Mr. Whatley if we can do shows in front of his candy store at the mall. If we put a little money box out front I bet we could make at least a hundred dollars a day, easy. I betcha by the time we're grown up we'll have our own television specials and—"

"Yeah, but...."

6.
Juggling

After teaching hundreds of students how to juggle, I've found that one's degree of success (with a few exceptions to be discussed later) is directly proportionate to one's enjoyment of juggling. If the first time you manage to keep three balls moving through the air your eyes don't go wide and you don't hear a little voice in your head say "Wow!," you'll know juggling isn't your area of Independent Entertainment. You should have as much fun juggling for yourself as you do for others.

Unlike the other forms of Independent Entertainment discussed in this book, juggling is the only skill that isn't inherently theatrical in nature. Juggling is a learned physical skill that happens to be interesting enough to be viewed by spectators. The juggler does not need the audience to pretend to believe or accept a stylized reality, but only to watch and marvel at his skills. Watching a juggling performance can be as pure and direct an experience as listening to jazz or classical music.

Of course, juggling is not limited to a "skills only" form of presentation. Most financially successful jugglers use their juggling skills as a base to which they add comedy and theatrics. These performers usually started out as simple jugglers who wanted to share their skills with an audience, and, once in front of an audience, found they needed to fill in the silence while juggling. They ended up becoming well-rounded entertainers. Funny how that works.

Other Independent Entertainers—mimes, clowns, magicians, and puppeteers—will find that being able to do five minutes or so of juggling will do more for their act than add time. Besides being entertaining in itself, the juggling will break the act into several short segments. This creates a pacing that will make it easier to keep an audience's attention.

HANDICAPS

One myth that needs to be destroyed is that "everyone and anyone" can learn to juggle. You will see this claim in every juggling book ever printed and hear it from every juggling instructor who would like your tuition money. These claims are more often the result of blind zeal than of guile. Once someone is juggling, he finds it so easy to do that he can't imagine anyone else not being able to juggle. According to research conducted at a Texas university, the truth is that about five to ten percent of the physically mature, healthy population are unable to juggle or can only juggle very poorly and with great effort. This is due to poor parallel vision. Parallel vision is the ability of the eye to track simultaneously separate objects in a field of space. Soccer and basketball players, who have to know in which direction the ball and other players are moving, have highly developed parallel vision. Would-be jugglers with poor parallel vision have a rough time ahead of them.

LEARNING

I taught myself to juggle. I had no partner, instructor, books or concepts of patterns. The disadvantage of this approach was that it took a long time to learn the skill. This disadvantage was offset by pursuing the very exciting, adventurous path of using my mind and imagination to discover new patterns and movements. It was fun enough that it never once seemed a slow process.

Learning to juggle from a book is certainly an interesting idea—and that's about it. I don't see how a raw beginner, someone who has no idea of what's going up or coming down, can apply the step-by-step written instructions to a workable pattern. The only positive effect a book can have is to provide a formalized *motivation* for picking up those three balls and *practicing!* With consistent practice and one or two hints, something is bound to happen.

A juggling book can be helpful to someone who knows how to juggle and is looking for a listing of further tricks and variations.

The quickest way to learn to juggle is from someone who knows, either in a class or on a one-to-one basis. The class situation is the most desirable since it offers you a chance to see and learn from a number of people.

PRACTICE

Some jugglers practice as many as twelve hours a day, especially when learning new patterns. While learning, you should plan on at least one hour a day of practice. Remember that skills are accumulated over time—you will not learn as much in one 7-hour day as you will in seven 1-hour days.

Practicing with music has proven valuable to many jugglers. Music provides an energy level and pacing with which to link juggling. At times, you'll find yourself sitting back, listening to the music, and watching the balls juggle all on their own—(well, almost anyway). It doesn't even feel like work.

After you've learned to juggle and have a fairly solid act worked out, how much should you practice? For the average Independent Entertainer, I suggest practicing as little as possible. Excess practice will sap you of the energy and enthusiasm needed for performing. Many performing musicians do the same—they find themselves doing their best work during practice sessions with an empty room as an audience.

The few jugglers who rely solely on highly developed juggling skills will of course need many hours of practice to maintain their skills, let alone learn new ones. Should you ever become this skilled, you'll probably be out of the realm of Independent Entertainment. You'll be what's known as "a big deal."

PROPS

How many props will you need? I've seen some jugglers execute a wonderful show with only three balls, and others who need a trailerful to perform a mediocre show. Most jugglers will try to get by with as many props as they can carry in a medium-sized backpack.

The juggler, fortunately, doesn't need to spend as much time building and buying props as do clowns and magicians. You can either build everything you need in a few afternoons or buy it all in

one shot from one of several different juggling supply houses.
Here's what you'll need:

Bean Bags Many beginning jugglers prefer to start with bean bags. They don't bounce away from you when they are dropped. Some people like the little "tcht, tcht, tcht" sound they make when caught. Bean bags can be very colorful and have pleasant textures—velvet, silk, and corduroy. They don't hurt much when they bounce off your eye. Bean bags make less of a "thwack" than hard rubber balls when dropped on the floor of your second-story apartment. Your neighbors will certainly applaud your decision to juggle with bean bags.

But there are drawbacks to bean bags. The most obvious is that they don't bounce when you want them to bounce. Not so obvious is that when juggling in a quick, tight, precise pattern, bean bags are a little too slow for comfort and accuracy. The filler (beans, popcorn, rice) absorbs a portion of the impact or thrust, thus slowing the elapsed time it takes to achieve the desired result. Outdoor use of bean bags is limited by the potentially damaging effect of dirt, mud, and water on the bags. Who wants to risk having their bean bags begin sprouting in middle of a performance?

Balls There is only one style of ball worthy of consideration: the lacrosse ball. It's a hard rubber ball that measures two and one half inches in diameter and weighs six ounces. It has a solid, true bounce. It fits in your hand like a dream. Where can you obtain this veritable godsend? Most sporting goods stores carry them. If not available, they can be ordered from juggling supply houses. (I don't doubt that more lacrosse balls are sold to jugglers than to players of the vicious game of lacrosse.) The price will run from one and half to two and a half dollars per ball.

Don't waste time juggling tennis balls, racquet balls, baseballs, sponge rubber balls, or any other inferior substitute. Thousands of jugglers have searched in vain for a substitute. Take it from them, there are none.

While you will likely start with three balls, I suggest buying six. You will probably never juggle six balls (though you'll be doing four and five sooner than you think), but you will frequently run into another juggler or anxious would-be juggler who has nothing to juggle. It's worth having an extra few balls to share with him when the time comes.

If you tire of the color of your lacrosse balls (they are made in white and dull orange), take two round balloons of the same color and wrap them over a ball. Wrap the second over the hole left by the first balloon. Do this to the other two balls and you've got something going.

Some jugglers use lacrosse balls for practice and larger balls (softball size) for performances. This is done with the intention of making it easier for audiences to see the objects. This might be helpful at a very large show (halftime shows at football games), but for most of the work you'll be doing as an Independent Entertainer it's not necessary. Your audience will be able to see just fine. Remember, large balls appear to move slower, small balls (lacrosse size) seem zippier and bubblier.

Rings Rings are made easily from one-quarter inch plywood. A comfortable size is fifteen and one-eighth inch outside diameter and thirteen and three-eighths inside diameter. After cutting the plywood with a sabersaw, file the splinters off the edges of the rings. Wrap them with colored plastic tape. Do not use plastic tape with thread or cloth binding. You'll need to stretch the tape to make it fit with no wrinkles, something you can do only with pure plastic tape.

If you have a few extra dollars to spend, you might invest in plastic rings. Either you can buy a sheet of Plexiglas and cut your own (risky and time-consuming), or you can order a set.

Plastic rings are nicer than plywood rings. Not only are they lighter and thinner, making them easier to carry, store, and juggle, but you can do tricks with them that you can't do with plywood rings. The most popular plastic ring trick is to catch a spinning ring in a ring held horizontally in your hand. The caught ring will continue spinning in a vertical position.

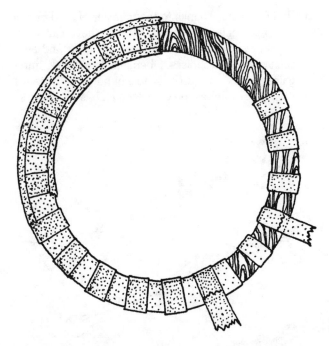

Fig. 13 Construction of a wooden ring

One is limited in the number of tricks to be done with rings because of their very nature. They have to be thrown vertically and with spin. They are large and not easily maneuvered. The best ring routines are those which emphasize the visual characteristics of the ring, not the juggler's skills. Try to achieve a floating, flying effect with rings. Juggle high and wide, covering a large space with your patterns.

For a finish that is guaranteed to open some eyes, flap the rings down over your head and onto your shoulders one-two-three!

Clubs The third most basic juggling prop is the club.

Fifty years ago, jugglers were using bowling pins and wooden Indian clubs. One old-time juggler told me he had broken two of his toes with bowling pins. Thanks to the miracles of modern science, jugglers no longer need quick feet. We now have clubs made of fiberglass and of polyethylene, the latter being far and away the more popular of the two choices. Fiberglass clubs crack, hurt when rapped against bones, and run close to a hundred dollars a set. The most you'll pay for the best polyethylene club is ten dollars.

Fig. 14
A. *Broomstick conversion*
B. *Molded fiberglass*
C. *Molded polyethylene with decorative trim*

If you are determined to hold on to every extra nickel (or, as in my case when first starting out, you don't have any extra nickels), you can make your own clubs. Cut a one-inch diameter broom handle into eighteen-or nineteen-inch lengths. Carve a hole two-thirds of the way through each of the three sponge rubber *baseball-sized* balls. The hole should be small enough to provide a good, tight fit when pushed over the end of a stick. Wrap the sticks with decorative plastic tape. I wrapped a thin layer of foam rubber beneath the tape at the handle of my club, thus preventing many a bashed knuckle.

You now have an attractive, very inexpensive, well-balanced juggling club. Combined with your extraordinary talents, your clubs will delight audiences time and time again. They're a bit heavy for fancy work, but good for the muscles in your arms. If you're smart, you'll take the money you earn with these clubs and buy a professionally built set. I regret that I didn't do so sooner than I did.

Scarves For one thin dollar bill, you can outfit yourself with three brand-new, brightly colored chiffon scarves, available at your nearest dimestore. Let one go in midair and watch it float s-l-o-w-l-y

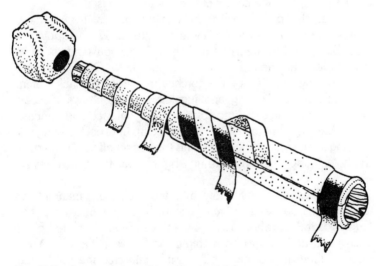

Fig. 15 Production stages of handmade club

to the ground. Isn't that fun? Surprisingly, it takes more effort to juggle scarves than other objects. In order to overcome the aerodynamic resistance, you have to throw them with vigor.

One nice effect is to grab a scarf by the corner and pull it through the air so it looks like a fast-moving line.

Torches and Other Fiery Objects Fire adds a distinctive element of mystery and danger to an act, providing something for your audience to remember easily. There is something hypnotizing about torches being juggled in the dark. The flame, being on the top two inches of a club, appears to move at varying speeds. One moment it floats stationary, and the next, as the club begins the second half of its revolution, the flame whips around with incredible speed. The dull, orange-red light from the flames gives the juggler's face an unearthly appearance.

Torches are the most commonly juggled flaming objects. I've only heard of a few people who juggle other objects. One person juggles fireballs while wearing asbestos gloves, and the other has a ball suspended in the center of each of three rings.

There is no real danger in juggling torches. If your hand comes into contact with the flame (produced by a wrapping of asbestos soaked in kerosene or lighter fluid), you tend to move away faster than the time its takes to burn flesh. One precaution: After soaking the tips of the torches in kerosene, shake them vigorously before lighting and juggling. You don't want excess drops of flaming kerosene to splatter onto your face and hands.

One juggler in Iowa City discovered an unexpected danger in juggling torches. The smoke from his torches set off the fire alarm in the hotel lobby where he was juggling. He was promptly arrested.

Cigar Boxes We move now into the realm of "manipulative juggling" (as opposed to "toss juggling"). One item used in toss juggling is the cigar box. You'll need three of them, one to hold in each hand and one to be manipulated between the two. You'll want to tape the lid shut and possibly reinforce the inside with styrofoam. Next, glue felt or sandpaper to the ends of the boxes to prevent them from slipping apart from each other.

As you might have guessed, you can buy "professional" cigar boxes. Fiberglass or carefully constructed wooden boxes with pigskin leather on the ends will run ten to fifteen dollars apiece. Hollow, molded plastic boxes are available for less.

How do you learn cigar box manipulation? After you've seen someone else operate them (surely by this time in your career you've seen a cigar box routine), you'll know what needs to be done. The big secret is to keep practicing. For an invigorating inspiration, keep an eye for W. C. Field's incredible cigar box routine in the film *The Old-Fashioned Way*.

Devil or Chinese Stick The devil stick runs anywhere from twenty-four to thirty inches in length, one inch wide at the ends, and is tapered to three-quarters of an inch in the center. It is wrapped with either friction tape or cloth bicycle tape. It is kept in motion in midair by hitting it with two twelve-inch wooden dowels, one held in each hand. The devil stick originated in Asia, hence it's other common name, the Chinese stick. You can purchase one for about ten dollars. If you have access to a wood lathe, you can easily make your own. Remember, the longer the stick, the slower it moves. It's a good idea for beginners to start with a thirty-inch stick.

You need only see the devil stick operated once to get the idea of what you need to do. Ah, but to get beyond the idea, many long hours are needed.

Etc., Etc., Other common objects to be juggled and manipulated include the yo-yo, diabolo (a sort of yo-yo that bounces off a taut string), spinning plates, hoop and parasol, baton, and the spinning rope. Collect and learn the operation of these objects at your leisure. They will become extras that you'll add to a basic, solid juggling routine of balls, rings, and clubs.

THE THREADS

The juggler is blessed with the option of choosing almost any style of clothing he wishes. The only qualifying factors are that the clothing isn't physically constricting and that the colors don't

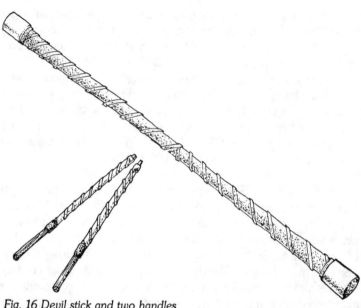

Fig. 16 Devil stick and two handles

interfere with the audience's view of the juggling. For instance, don't wear a black leotard top and juggle black balls.

In more commercial environments, jugglers have traditionally worn tuxedoes or sequined jumpsuits. More recently, however, many jugglers have begun to wear informal, casual, and fun clothing. This represents a sincere effort on their part to make juggling less flashy and stupendous and more natural and fun. Many newer jugglers, especially the Independent Entertainers, want to make audiences feel closer to them by looking more informal and, therefore, more approachable. After pricing tuxedoes and custom-made sequined jumpsuits, I'm sure you'll agree that the casual, informal approach to clothing is most desirable.

THE JUGGLER'S AUDIENCE

Contrary to popular belief, the juggler's best audience is not a group of children. The most appreciative audiences are adults. They understand the difficulty of juggling and can share in an educated, mature appreciation of the aesthetic qualities of juggling. Adults may not always make as much noise as kids, but you'll find noise isn't always what you're after. Kids don't enjoy your juggling as much as they enjoy being involved in a happening.

One of my first shows was for a class of kindergarten children. I though they would be screaming and yelling when they saw me juggle three, four, and five balls through the air. Ha! They stared at me with their mouths open and faces blank. They clapped only when their teacher told them to clap. I left the classroom quietly and was never invited back.

It seems that until a child is eight or nine years old he or she has difficulty following the course of objects. The eye first learns to track objects horizontally, then vertically, and finally in arcs. This is always a handy, scientific-sounding explanation to rationalize the failure of one of your shows.

You're pretty safe if you gear your act toward adults. If adults enjoy it, chances are children will, too. An act that is geared to children, however, doesn't stand as much of a chance of going over well with adults. This applies to most forms of Independent Entertainment.

"NOW FOR THREE IN ONE HAND! I CAN DO THIS FOR HOURS, FOLKS, JUST WATCH!"

Be very careful not to bore your audiences. While your first few triple high spins with a double pirouette will elicit sounds of awe and admiration, fifteen or twenty such spins will elicit sincere yawns. Pay attention to your audience. Don't rely solely on applause as an indicating factor; sometimes your audience will be so engrossed in what you are doing that they won't think to applaud. The experience of a dozen shows will give you an idea of proper pacing and duration. The best advice I can offer is to keep your individual patterns, as well as your entire routine, on the short side. It's better to leave them wanting more than to risk boring them. If they really want to see more, they'll be at your next performance.

WOOPS!

So you dropped a few props? Big deal. Don't worry about it. The less it bothers you, the less it will bother your audience. If you frown and grimace each time you drop an object, your audience will feel uncomfortable and hold their breaths, hoping, for your sake as well as theirs, that you don't drop another one.

Magicians and jugglers are both in undesirable positions when it comes to mistakes. The performing musician may miss a note or two, and no one will notice. The actor can cover an improper inflection or movement. But when the magician or juggler blows a trick, there's no covering it up. The best you can do is make a joke out of it and quickly move on to the next part of your act. Sometimes I've performed a juggling routine and made no mistakes. This forces me to drop a ball intentionally so that I can throw in a few humorous "mistake" jokes.

Beyond the jokes, there's another possible advantage to making a few mistakes in juggling. It's been my experience in talking after shows with members of some audiences that they actually *liked* seeing me do something less than perfect by dropping a few props. Making mistakes apparently creates the feeling that what I'm doing is very difficult and that my attempts to do it are "human," as opposed to the often alienating machine-like perfection of other jugglers they have seen. Then again, there are members of the audience who will tell you that all you need is a little more practice.

There are jugglers, myself included, who, when doing their last trick (usually the most impressive), will intentionally flub it up two or three times before successfully completing it. This not only gives the performer a chance to go through the motions of a difficult trick a few times before putting himself on the line, but it also helps to build the suspense and impress on the audience how difficult the trick is (or how difficult he wants them to think it is).

One final word on mistakes—at all costs avoid causing injury to spectators. You will often find yourself working under some very crowded, cramped conditions with poor lighting. In these situations, don't do your more difficult routines where a mistake might cause a rapidly twirling club to fly in the wrong direction and draw blood, bruises, or tears. Of course, if your audience is more busy eating pizza than watching you, a few wildly thrown objects will quickly command their utmost attention.

"HEY! WHAT DO YOU THINK YOU'RE DOING, JUGGLING?"

Before, and especially after, shows you will invariably have some very demanding people asking you to "just juggle a few things for me." I say unto thee, resist! You are not a casual show-off juggler, you are a Professional Entertainer. Casual juggling is permissible only in casual surrounding such as in your home, in a park, or at juggling get-togethers. It is never permissible in your place of employment. Your employers will appreciate and admire this attitude and practice, as will your audiences.

Not only does casual juggling deteriorate your appearance to audiences by lessening the mystique of the performance, it will affect your own character and attitude. In treating juggling as an elite, special skill that has very specific and special times and conditions under which it is to be practiced and performed, you cannot help but consider yourself a thoughtful, dedicated professional. You must hold your performance skills in the highest esteem to be able to withstand the many hard times and self-doubts you'll face as an Independent Entertainer.

"HOW DOES HE DO THAT?"

Carol's eyes were spinning and her mouth hung open. She was awestruck by the street juggler's manipulations. "How does he do that, Bob?"

"Mmmm," responded Bob, as nonchalantly as possible. He didn't particularly feel like talking. It was not so much because his mouth was filled with a tasteless hot dog, but because, darnit, this was his first date with Carol and here she was ogling this juggler jerk!

"This guy's something else, isn't he, Bob? I mean, he's not only good, he's great. He makes it look so beautiful and charming. Ohhh! Did you see what he did? Now that was clever."

Bob swallowed his hot dog and got down to business. "There's all kind of guys who do acts on the streets in this area. A whole lotta jugglers that this guy could learn a thing or two from."

For the first time, Carol took her eyes away from the juggler. "Really? I wouldn't think there'd be that many. At least not that were this good."

"If he was one of the good ones, he'd be working Vegas or Tahoe or—"

Carol glanced back at the juggler and "WOW! Look what he'd doing now, I can't believe it!" She turned to find Bob's face, but he was wandering around. "Bob, what are you doing?"

"Hmm? Oh, just looking for a trash can for this napkin. I finished my hot dog."

"Well come look what he's doing, he's got these—oh ... I guess he finished that. I never thought any juggler could do a thing like that."

"Hey, these jugglers do all kinds of crazy things."

"But this wasn't crazy, it was—"

"That's all these guys do all their lives, you know? I mean, they're like machines."

Carol frowned and considered this line of thought. "I hadn't looked at it that way, especially when he makes it look so flowing and personal and just, oh, I don't know, just so pretty!"

"He probably does the same act with the same tricks and cute little smiles ten times a day. It can't help but look smooth and polished."

"You don't think he does it that often, do you?"

"At least. Probably more."

"Oh dear. He must get awfully ... Bob! Look what he's going to do! Bob, what if he hurts himself? Oh, it would be so ugly. Maybe we should stop him."

"C'mon, Carol, that's probably the easiest trick he does. You don't think he'd do any—holyjumpingsonofa—!!! ... Uh, heh, heh.

He took you in on that one for a second. He must do that to make it look real hard. That's gotta be it."

A look of gloom and perhaps even embarrassment crossed over Carol's face. "No. You don't think he'd fake a thing like that, do you? Just for applause?"

"Hey, it's like I was saying, these guys do this stuff at least ten times a day, day after day. How genuine can those smiles and jokes be after the seven hundredth time? And you don't really think he'd risk doing anything dangerous that many times, do you? Nah, these guys are sharp operators, real sharp."

"Gee, I feel kinda sorry for the guy. Don't you?"

"Sure I do, sure I do. Could you imagine dedicating your life to throwing a bunch of things around in the air and telling a bunch of old, tired jokes? No thanks."

Carol moved closer to Bob. For the first time, she took his hand. "As sad as it is, it's still a special talent, don't you think? I mean, not everyone can do that."

"No, that's why they train seals and bears to juggle stuff around, cuz not everyone wants to waste their time. Most people got brains to do something more with their lives."

Carol squeezed his hand. "You want to go now?"

"Go now? But the guy hasn't finished his act."

"I guess I've seen enough. There are other things we can do."

"Sure."

After they turned the corner, Carol found a used bookstore she wanted to investigate.

"Yeah, okay," said Bob, "go on in. I'm gonna run back and grab another hot dog. I'll be back in a few minutes."

Bob ran back to where the juggler had been performing. He had finished his act and was putting away his props. "Hey, uh, juggler."

The juggler looked up and smiled at Bob.

"Uh, listen," said Bob. "You think you could show me how to juggle real quick like? Man, I'd give anything to be able to do what you do."

7.
Getting Your Act Together

Previous chapters have dealt only with performance skills as they related specifically to particular forms of Independent Entertainment. More often than not, while these comments are applied specifically to individual forms, they will be applicable to almost all forms. For example, information given to the juggler might also come in handy for the puppeteer.

This chapter presents an in-depth study of general performance behavior.

SMILE! SMILE! SMILE!

When your objective is to make people happy, it's good to know that smiles are contagious. Be friendly. Your audiences will appreciate it, you'll feel good, and your employers can't help but think they're getting their money's worth. Happy faces and laughs are the most concrete proof there is that you're having a positive effect on your audience. This is not to say that you can't produce any other effect on your audience and not be considered successful, only that smiles are the most frequently desired effect and financially rewarding.

This is a good point to which both clowns and jugglers should pay particular attention. The sad-faced tramp clown may get the initial bookings, but the repeat shows will be slow coming. "We decided to hire Mr. Giggles—kids have the *greatest* time with him."

Be friendly in your verbal approach to audiences, too. Usually you will be working close to them in informal atmospheres that are not well-suited to sarcasm, satire, and abrasive conduct.

INDEPENDENT ENTERTAINMENT AND FREEDOM OF EXPRESSION

The Independent Entertainer who strives for financial success would do well to follow one very general rule—be an entertainer first, a propagandist second. This isn't saying you have no business expressing your ideas, only that your first objective is to be entertaining. Financial success will be a long way off if you express your ideas (political, social, religious, and so on) at the expense of providing "good times" for your audience.

Your audience is generally going to be relaxed, casual, and informal. Frequently, they are not even expecting to be entertained. People in these audiences are not especially disposed to considering your views on the ramifications of post-Jungian psychology or the morality of abortion. They want to have fun. You are most likely to make the most amount of money by satisfying that desire.

But wait a moment. Suppose your views on nuclear power, for example, are important to you. Very important. Suppose you think there should be some overall legal and moral change made by society in regard to nuclear power. Shouldn't you use your entertainment skills to express your attitudes and attempt to cause others to think like you? If it's important to you, yes.

Ah, but how, in an entertaining, nonalienating manner, can you communicate complex, controversial and/or abstract ideas to an unsuspecting, frequently uncaptive audience?

The first thing to remember is that you aren't going to change the world with even as many as a hundred performances. At best, you'll be lucky to alter the perception of a few individuals on a subject or two. Stanley Kramer, a film director renown for his intense, dramatic films dealing with a variety of social and psychological problems, was once asked if he felt frustrated that his films didn't cause significant change. He replied that his primary concerns were to entertain his audience and to express, for his own satisfaction, his own ideas. If even as many as one or two people per thousand, he continued, walked out of a theater after seeing one of his films and said as much as "Gee, I never thought of it quite like that before," he would think it a wonderful thing—but not the most important.

Being aware that any change you create will be very small should indicate the best approach in communicating potentially troublesome (troublesome, that is, for your audience to accept during your performance) ideas. Be subtle in your approach. Those who blurt out blunt rhetoric either quickly alienate the average audience or end up performing for those who are already sympathetic to their ideas.

Subtlety is a great challenge for the bulk of Independent Entertainers. Performing on noisy street corners to passersby, in pizza parlors to partygoers, at fraternal organizations to the stauncher establishment—all are difficult situations for the Independent Entertainer who wants to do more than grab a few cheap laughs.

Work with the advantages unique to Independent Entertainment. Performing for small, informal crowds can give you the chance to search out individual faces and focus on those whom you think are most likely to listen and react. And when people are relaxed and rolling along with everything you throw at them, not expecting to be "worked on," their resistance to propaganda is probably very low. This makes it easier for you to insert both directly and indirectly—some of your ideas. Members of the audience will keep on nodding their heads and laughing, not actually realizing that they've been gently nudged into thinking more along the lines you want them to think.

SITUATIONS TO GET YOURSELF INTO

There are three basic situations in which an Independent Entertainer will find himself working: formal, casual, and of course, that wonderful hodgepodge, the in-between. When you first start out, you will work in each of these situations. As your career progresses, you may possibly find it best to concentrate on only one area.

Your first jobs will likely be casual situations. You'll be walking around at small craft festivals, fairs, and other places where you can meander and do your stuff for audiences of only one or two. Or, maybe you'll stand in one place and let the one's and two's walk past you.

Casual situations are both easy and difficult to perform successfully. The biggest problem beginners have to face is trying to get the same results from a casual situation that they would get from a formal situation. It doesn't happen. People will generally watch you for five or ten minutes and then move on, often walking away in the middle of a routine. Casual shows receive casual attention.

Concentrating on the advantages unique to a particular situation makes the problems less worrisome. Don't bother developing a "performance" atmosphere. Be like everyone else at the function and relax and have fun. If you're a clown, just talk to kids and whomever else wants to talk to you. Your clown character will shine. Jugglers and magicians, go ahead and perform your tricks, but make sure that you find plenty of time to talk to people about your art and whatever else happens to pop up. Mimes, take requests. Find victims for your mirror image routine. Puppeteers, let your puppets have discussions with people. They'll like nothing better than to tell their friends, "Oh, I talked to the nicest puppet today!"

Be personable with your audience. They'll like receiving the exclusive attention and you'll appreciate the relaxed, natural, unpressured opportunity for your stage character to expand and mature. You will also appreciate being able to relate to your audience as individuals. There are many Independent Entertainers, particularly clowns, who enjoy working in casual sitautions more than any others.

There usually isn't much of a problem in getting jobs for casual occasions. Your employer, anxious to add atmosphere to an event will be more than happy to have you.

Formal situations are those in which you perform before an attentive, captive audience. Most commonly, you will find yourself performing to a seated audience on a stage or a stage area. This includes anything from a concert to a backyard birthday party. In any case, the structure of your act is the same; it has a beginning, a middle, and an ending.

Most Independent Entertainers prefer formal situations. Because audiences are geared to be very attentive, they are more likely to be appreciative of your skills and more enthusiastic in their expression of that appreciation.

Performing in formal situations is pleasing to the ego for other reasons, too. It makes most Independent Entertainers feel very successful and professional to be the unchallenged center of attention. They frequently find that they do their best work in these situations. Directing and funneling the audience's energy into the act will enable the performer to do better than he knew he could do.

Unfortunately, many Independent Entertainers don't let formal work stop at being pleasing to the ego; they allow it to spoil the ego. "Stage work is all I want to do. I'm *too good* to be doing pizza parlors and birthday parties!" It's a real downer for these people when they can't find any formal situations to work in and have to start scrounging around again for birthday parties. When you're not working, you're not an entertainer. You're unemployed. Never consider yourself too good for any type of job situation. Only allow yourself to consider some types of jobs to be more desirable than others.

The in-between situations are the lifeblood of the Independent Entertainer. They include every situation that is neither strictly formal nor casual. The prime example of an in-between performance situation is working in a pizza parlor. Your audience is half-watching you and half-eating. And they'll be talking while you're doing a half formally structured act (beginning, middle, and end) and a half casually structured act (taking a minute here and there to talk with kids or doing a quick little routine directed only at one particularly appreciative tableful of people).

It's rough, but it's fun. You're on your toes every minute. Each instant you're planning for the next: Should I stand over here or over there? Should I talk louder so everyone can hear me or should I go to the other side and repeat this skit? Should I talk to this little girl? Should I have some fun with that heckler or ignore him? Should I do the next skit now or take a break and let 'em finish their dinners? And what should I do with this little kid who's been trying to kick me in the shins for the last ten minutes? Never a dull moment.

In casual, nonpressure situations, you need to be fairly low key and easy-going. In a formal situation, you go on stage, perform your act and walk off. But in in-between situations, you're never sure *what* is going to happen during the show, how you'll do it, which direction it'll take, or where it'll end up. You learn to think on your feet. I think this is the greatest thrill for the Independent Entertainer. It puts excitement and variety into the act, forcing the performer to use his greatest asset, his mind. A performer who succeeds in these situations is likely to succeed in other forms of entertainment as well. He'll succeed because he's a thinker, not because he happens to know particular performance tricks and skills.

Your mind is your best tool. Use it.

WHERE YOU'RE AT

You will often have something to say about the arrangement of the stage area and audience. Exercise this power to your advantage. Cram the most people into the smallest area possible, as close to the stage as you can. The closer people are to each other, the more enthusiasm and noise will be generated. The bigger the hall, the smaller (or more "intimidated") the audience will feel. The further away from you they are, even if packed closely together, the slower their reaction time will be. I've seen a regular one-hour show run an extra thirty minutes once when the stage was fifty feet from the audience.

When working in restaurants and other tightly packed areas, get to the show early and move some tables around so you have a place in which to work that is both safe and visible. Don't let the junior assistant manager, in an effort to exercise authority, stop you from doing what you have to do to guarantee a successful show. Junior assistants and other underlings tend to be afraid of anything "different."

THE SPICE OF LIFE

Variety within the act is not only the Independent Entertainer's spice of life, it's a good way to increase potential earnings. Nobody likes to see the same show year after year.

The first telltale sign that your act is getting old and in need of a few new routines is when you begin to hear members of the audience whisper "Watch this! Watch what he does now!" This doesn't mean they won't enjoy what's coming up, only that they've seen it a few times. If they see it many more times, though, you'll hear, "Poor guy, stuck doing the same old thing for the rest of his life. Tsk, tsk." Don't laugh—it happens to many entertainers.

And it might happen to you. You've put a lot of hours, days, maybe even years into developing what you think is a good, solid act. You've spent a lot of money on props and costumes. You've finally got enough bookings to keep you happy. You're even managing to put a little bit of money into your savings account. Ah, success at long last! Now you can sit back, relax, and reap the rewards from your earlier efforts. "Hey, I've paid my dues. Why shouldn't I sit back?" There are lots of reasons why you shouldn't.

An Independent Entertainer never quits paying dues. You must *always* be improving, changing, and modifying your routine to maximize financial earnings. Always. Saying "I'll work on some new material, oh, sometime after next Christmas" doesn't cut the mustard—unless you happen to be so fortunate as to be booked solid through Christmas.

Continually modifying and adding to your act keeps your mind active. You will be thinking forward and growing. You won't find yourself getting bored with the same old routine. Boredom causes you to work with less enthusiasm, which in turn encourages even more boredom and disinterest. This is the beginning of the end.

If you can't tell when you're getting bored, or think you can cover it up, your audience can't and won't be deceived. Even if they haven't seen your routine eleven times in two months, they'll sense it's old, stale, and tired. Oh, they'll laugh and applaud, but there will begin to be a few less effervescent comments to your employer and to you after the show. There will be fewer invitations to perform at other events. The final result will be less dollars in your pocket.

It's a job. Why not work at it full time like you would at any other?

AND THEN THERE'S VERSATILITY

I've referred to variety as the constant modification, improvement, and change of a particular act. It is also the ability to perform different acts in various forms of Independent Entertainment. This type of versatility in Independent Entertainment is both personally and financially rewarding and doesn't require the amount of effort you might think. It certainly doesn't require all the work that it took to learn your first field of Independent Entertainment.

Suppose you've got a nice, tight, juggling routine worked out that has plenty of verbal humor and audience rapport. You've worked with both children and adults. You're earning a regular income, and people know your name. Since things are finally going so good for you, why not make them go better?

You seem to be fairly dextrous at handling props, so why not learn some magic tricks? Come to think of it, since becoming a juggler, you've gained a lot of confidence in your ability to control your body. Why not attend a mime class this quarter at a local college? In three or four months, you'll be performing mime and magic shows that are as impressive as your juggling act.

I know what you're thinking—"It took me almost a year to get where I am with juggling, how can I learn the other skills any faster?" Because juggling has paved the way for you to diversify your talents, that's how.

You've already gone through the process of learning an entertainment skill. You should now know how to practice much more efficiently. And with your success in juggling, you have a solid idea of what the rewards of that practice will be, giving you the added incentive to work even harder than you did at juggling. You'll also know better than to waste time and money on inferior props. At the start, you'll get the best props for your needs.

In designing your performances, you'll know precisely the types of audiences you'll be performing for and what sort of material they would like to see. It took you a while to understand audiences, didn't it. There's no need to spend time and energy worrying about those things now, is there?

The confidence you've gained in relating publicly to people will encourage you to start performing mime and magic a lot sooner than you did juggling. Remember how you insisted that you wouldn't juggle in public until you could do five balls? And how after a few frustrating months you gave *that* up and finally performed? You now know that the sooner you jump in and perform mime and magic, the faster you'll improve.

If you want to, you can schedule five magic shows for next week and at least that many for your mime act. Your juggling career has given you good connections and a fine reputation. You know who to talk to and what they need.

Come to think of it, why not put together a casual sort of clown act? And if you could only find someone to make some puppets for you....

DRAWING THE BIG GOOSE EGG (THAT IS, BOMBING)

It happens to the best of entertainers, so don't let the prospect of bombing freeze your blood. Like it or not, there will be times when you won't be able to buy as much as a timid giggle. Sometimes it's your fault, sometimes it's the audience's fault, other times it's no one's fault.

The first time you bomb (disregarding your learning performance), you're most likely to feel terrible. "I'm no good. I stink. Who do I think I am, anyway, standing in front of these strangers and telling these dumb puppet stories?" You'll even feel bad about accepting payment for your performance.

Once you are away from the show and on your way home, you'll start rerunning the catastrophe in your head: "Where did I go wrong? Maybe I should have talked louder. Maybe I should have moved closer to the audience. Maybe I should shorten each routine." Examine thoroughly everything you did: how, why, when, where. Be harsh, be cruel, but find out what you did wrong.

Once you're at home, safe in your familiar sanctuary of privacy and security, you might easily start thinking "The setting wasn't quite right. It was pitch black (it was lit, you just didn't have a 10,000 watt spotlight), the acoustics weren't right (you're forgetting that you've worked successfully on street corners at rush hour), and I didn't have an elevated stage (there were only twenty-five people and each of them had a clear view). No wonder the show fell flat."

By the time you get in bed that night, you'll realize it wasn't your fault at all! You had nothing to do with the fact that you bombed. It was *them.* "They just don't appreciate quality when they see it. Not everyone does. If anyone should be embarrassed about anything, *they* should be embarrassed for his or her ignorance of intelligence in a puppet production. Ha! That's the last time I'll ever consent to perform for *them!"*

Give it some time, and a few more not-so-successful shows, and you'll begin to gain some honest perspective on the situation of bombing. Your poor results are probably a varied mixture of all three causes: you, them, and the setting. You may have given a duplicate performance of your usual knock 'em, rock 'em show, but that one night the audience did not respond. This doesn't automatically mean it was the audience's fault—it could very well *still* be yours. You should have seen that you had to make adjustments to suit their fancy. It's your responsibility to entertain, not theirs to be entertained.

Suppose you did try to adjust and nothing happened. In that case, the problem could lie with the audience. Maybe there was a large enough group of people enough out of phase with your act that their lack of enthusiasm spread to others. They may have been too old, too young, too tired, too hot, too cold, too anything to be able to connect with you, or you with them. Funny thing is, you could give a duplicate performance to the same group of people on another night and have them jumping out of their seats.

When you have a quiet audience, concentrate on the most attentive, enthusiastic group of people you can find and hope the energy will spread to the others.

The setting of the show can also be an important factor. In addition to the size of the area relative to the size of the audience, and the distance of the stage to the audience, factors such as lighting, extraneous noise, time of day, day of the week, and even the temperature can affect audience response.

The best time to bomb is when you start walking and talking a little too cocky as a result of your success in Independent Entertainment. Bombing teaches you that you can never take your success for granted. You've got to be on your toes and *work* for success in each and every performance.

In rare instances, bombing can be a growing experience for your performance skills. When nothing is happening in the way of clapping, laughing, and other responses, and you realize that nothing you can do will change the response, what have you got to lose? Perhaps it's a defense mechanism, but on a few occasions when I've bombed, I've found myself letting loose and doing all kinds of loud, brassy, outlandish things—things I would never do otherwise. It's almost a dare to the audience to see if they'll respond to *anything*. As long as you aren't sarcastic or blatantly disrespectful to the audience, there's nothing wrong with this sort of behavior.

Another funny thing about bombing is that sometimes when you think you've bombed, you haven't. I've given shows to audiences who have been dead quiet. After those shows, I've had an inordinate amount of people personally compliment me and tell me how thoroughly they enjoyed my act. It is a confusing situation, but one of which you should be aware. Verbal and physical audience response does not necessarily equal audience appreciation.

But try as you might, you can't always avoid failure. When it happens, learn from it and move on with no regrets or hesitation. As you gain experience, you'll learn to analyze and determine ahead of time the possibility of bombing at a particular show. Avoiding risky performances is smart thinking—unless you happen to need the income and don't think a bad show will hurt future earning potential.

WORKING UNINDEPENDENTLY

Working with a partner or an assistant may open up new possibilities for your act, but it will definitely impose some limitations and risks. In most cases, I strongly advise against having another person become an integral part of your act.

The only factors in favor of working with another person are that you might enjoy his or her company, and that you enjoy sharing your entertaining experiences with another person. Some people just aren't cut out to be loners—they need the constant support found in companionship. The skits and routines you'll work up with another person won't be any better than what you could do on your own, but they will be different, easier, and more fun to develop.

The disadvantages of working with others are many and important. What if your partner gets sick and you have to cancel a performance? What if he or she doesn't think the two of you should give a particular performance that you want to do? What if he or she accepts a performance date for less money than you want to work for? Will you be able to double your fee when you add a partner? (Ha!) Will it ruin your friendship if you decide to split the partnership? Are you willing to share the spotlight? Is he or she willing to share the burdens?

You might be considering the use of an assistant (as opposed to a partner). A good assistant will take orders, won't argue, provide company, help you set up and tear down quickly, and move props on and off the stage during the performance. An assistant can even be incorporated into two-person routines. With an assistant, you can have all the advantages of working with a partner and working alone rolled into one.

Unfortunately, even good assistants don't last long. The fun of being on stage soon wears thin, and the trifling salary you pay (if you bother paying anything) is no guarantee of loyalty. If your assistant happens especially to enjoy being on stage, he or she probably has a plan or two in the works.

Despite the possible advantages an assistant offers, you will still need to expend new and additional time and effort in worrying about his or her performance, arrival times, departure times, and maintenance of happiness on the job. You'll have to manage another person. Not only that, you won't be paid to manage your assistant. My experience has been that I would rather work twice as hard alone than carry the unprofitable burden of being to any degree, responsible for and dependent on another person.

Should you ever decide to work with a partner or partners, keep it on a fun-only basis. Don't regard it as a business, or depend on it as an income with which to pay the bills. I frequently work with juggling partners at casual events, but only because I happen to enjoy the opportunity to pass clubs with others. It's not even important to me that I get paid.

HANG TIME

After you've finished your show at the pizza parlor, there's nothing more tempting than to sit down and eat a freebie pizza. I don't mean to spoil your appetite, but don't do it. This applies particularly to entertainers in elaborate costume, notably mimes and clowns. Becoming one with the audience weakens your image. Kids will begin to wonder if you're a real clown or just a person. Bad news.

If you do decide to eat that pizza or piece of birthday cake, do it only when accomplishing some public relations work. It'll give you a chance to chitchat comfortably with your employer and with anyone else who feels it important to talk to the star of the moment.

BABY-SITTING

"Say, we were having a big party this weekend and we though we could use you to entertain the kids for a couple of hours. How about it?" This query translates into: "Will you baby-sit the kids and keep them out of our hair?"

This is not the type of situation in which you want to get yourself involved. Make sure your clients understand that you are a *professional* and that they respect your position. Don't get caught in a baby-sitting spot. If it sounds like it might turn into that—"C'mon over around noon and we'll see what happens"—tell your prospective employer that you need a precise starting time. Be firm. Make it clear that you want the kids to be sitting still in one spot waiting for you to perform.

No entertainer can pretend to keep children entertained for as long as an hour. Attempts to do so tend to make the entertainer look like a failure, both to the children who get bored with him and to the adult who is paying. The only place to work long hours is where there is a steady stream of fresh faces.

There are "entertainers" who specialize in baby-sitting, especially at birthday parties. For a fee, they'll bring cake and other foods, organize games, songs, and even wash the dirty dishes. If you have even the slightest bit of talent as an entertainer, you don't need to pursue this option.

WHO ME? COMPLAIN?

Who wants to watch an enjoyable, uplifting, fun performance by a wonderful entertainer, only to talk to him after the show and find out he leads a glum, bum life? Nobody wants to hear you tell them how difficult your lifestyle is, how little money you might have, your problems in obtaining bookings, or the raunchy audiences you have to perform for.

Your conversation with audience members, employers, and even your friends should always be enthusiastic and optimistic. When someone asks you how business is going, the only answer is "Couldn't be better, couldn't be better."

You're an entertainer and your purpose is to make people happy. Tell them what makes them the happiest. Besides, when you get right down to it, it's none of their business what your financial status or personal life is like.

I had an acquaintence who was always asking my closer friends what kind of money I was earning. He was dying to know. My friends couldn't really tell him anything (they didn't know), so one day he finally popped the question to me. "Gee, Happy, what do you get paid for one of your concert shows?" I replied that I received my usual fee. "What's that?" he wanted to know. I told him it varied from show to show. He finally got the idea and moved on to another subject.

The brighter the picture you paint of yourself and your business, the more successful people will think you are. And the more successful they think you are, the more they will want you to perform at their functions and the more they will be willing to pay you. It's a law of physics. Hollywood frequently pays famous stars millions to perform in a movie because the star is famous—not necessarily because he or she is a good actor. An actor's fame is due in large part to good public relations work.

"HEY, REALLY, WHAT DO YOU THINK OF MY ACT?"

As a beginner and an experienced professional, you'll be anxious to receive thoughtful, verbalized feedback from individuals. Finding and listening intelligently to good criticism, though, is a difficult thing to do.

Most people will tell you only what they think you want to hear— "It was great!" If people do comment on things they didn't like about your act, the odds are that you'll either take it personally or find a way to ignore it— "They don't know what they're talking about." Sadly, this is the case with many Independent Entertainers.

Perhaps the biggest key to making use of criticism is not to worry or be insulted or embarrassed by the specific items mentioned, but to concentrate on the individual's theory and basis of criticism and entertainment. Try to determine for yourself what his standards of good entertainment are. Learn to understand where your audience is coming from, even more so than they do. With this knowledge in hand, you, along with the response from the audience as a whole, will be the final judge of which specifics in your act are of good quality and which aren't.

**8.
Places
to Be**

BEFORE YOU DECIDE TO PERFORM THERE

There are a limitless number of places and situations in which you can perform. Before deciding to give a particular performance, it is wise to analyze the precise reason why you are giving the performance. Do not surrender your ability to think, reason, and evaluate to the blind dictate of "Perform for the sake of performing!" Granted, you are eager to perform, but you are not an automaton. Even if you do decide to accept every single opportunity to do your act, make sure you have a specific reason for each separate performance.

The first reason behind many beginners' performances is the opportunity to learn. Until you've learned a skill, you can't really perform for any other purpose. As a beginner, you'll want to learn to execute a show smoothly with no embarrassing pauses or blunders, determine which pieces of material the audiences like, and all the other necessary entertaining skills you'll be using.

As an experienced professional, you'll still find yourself performing to learn, although only on rare occasions—such as when trying out a new piece of material prior to a big show, performing for a unique type of audience (deaf children, for example), or for any other reason.

The most common, most important reason for performing is financial profit. This does not mean your joy and satisfaction in performing and practicing an art form has been traded in for money. You haven't sold out. You've only come to the decision that you value highly your abilities and that you are not going to give them away for nothing. You want something back in fair exchange.

Of course, performing as an Independent Entertainer may be a hobby in which you dabble without concern for money. Your reason for performing is simple enough—fun. There is a wealthy juggler in Los Angeles who occasionally performs for movie theater lines. At the end of the show, he doesn't pass a hat around, *he hands out dollar bills.* He rather enjoys the looks on people's faces.

Even as a full-time professional, you made decide to give shows for fun and not for learning or profit. As I mentioned earlier, I frequently perform with other jugglers as part of a group because I enjoy the experience. Don't think for an instant, though, that if I had the opportunity to perform for profit elsewhere, I wouldn't.

COMPETING WITH YOURSELF

Don't let your early enthusiasm for performing prompt you to perform uninvited and informally. For instance, don't walk through the midway at the local county fair doing your juggling tricks when there's a chance you could have arranged to perform on the bandstand.

When those who do see you performing like this decide at a later date to hire a professional entertainer, they'll pass you by without thinking twice. They want someone special, not some local yokel amateur who practices in public.

TAKE IT TO THE STREETS

Ah, the streets! Throughout history, the streets have served as a perfect stage for the Independent Entertainer. There's alway's an audience and always an opening on stage (with exceptions). There is no place else an Independent Entertainer can gain so much experience in so short a time for so little an expenditure. You can, if the people are there, perform for twelve or fourteen hours a day. Even nicer, the only arrangements you'll have to make for the performance is the transportation.

Well, not quite. The government has decided to get into the act, too. This is the combined result of government's inherent nature to regulate whatever is unregulated and the self-serving, greedy, monopolistic interests of established street performers who don't want any competition. In many cities, one is now required to purchase a license for the right to perform and entertain on the streets. There is usually a limited number of licenses available, thus creating a government-sanctioned and enforced monopoly, with a very long list of applicants. Sadly, Independent Entertainers have been fined and threatened with arrest for performing without a license.

If you've called the city hall in your town and learned that no such license is required (darnit, now you've given them the idea), don't think you're off free and easy. Law enforcement officials, troubled by anything out of the ordinary and particularly by a probable nonmonied, nonpropertied, nomadic interest, will stop you in the middle of a performance, even though they have no power to do so. (Actually, they have the power—it's the right they don't have.) The most frequently used line they'll throw at you is something on the order of "It's illegal to beg or solicit donations on public streets without a permit." But gee willikers, officer, I can't help it if people drop money into my hat. I just like telling these puppet stories and doing—"I don't write the laws, kid, I just enforce them. Now beat it, and there won't be any problems. *Now.*" Yes, officer.

Should you be so unfortunate as to live in a city where the police aren't in the audience applauding, try the old hit-and-run approach. Do quick ten-minute routines where people are waiting for the bus or are in line to see a movie. Quickly pass the hat and move on to the next location.

MALLS: STREETS OF CARPET AND MUZAK

I speak here of privately owned, roofed and carpeted malls, not the renovated downtown outdoor malls which fall into the category of street work. Malls can be weird places for Independent Entertainers to work in. A mall is a multimillion dollar complex designed specifically to serve the needs of the world's largest commercial retail businesses. They are not designed to suit the needs of the very small, individually owned and operated businesses of Independent Entertainment.

Some malls, particularly in areas where there are several in competition with each other, strive to create a unique atmosphere. If the desired atmosphere is a fun and partylike one, there could be room for you and your act. Contact the public relations director of the mall. Approached in a professional manner, this person will listen to any offer that might potentially increase the number of shoppers at the mall. Do not, under any circumstances, perform without some kind of official clearance. The security guard will quickly whisk you away, and, when you finally do seek official clearance, your name will be remembered in an unfavorable light.

And have a lot of fun competing with that ever so zippy background music you'll find at every mall in the world

FAIRS

There are two distinct types of fairs: little and big. Little fairs include local craft displays, children's festivals, and other small one- or two-day-get-togethers. These are situations in which it's relatively easy to get a paying job, or at least permission to perform for contributions. The atmosphere is very pleasant and the people are friendly and easy to please. Little fairs offer many opportunities for the beginner.

Big fairs are another story. Plan on making your business arrangements with the fair board and its commissioner months ahead of time. They have already booked adult entertainment (probably country and western music), so now they are probably looking for something for the kids. Even though you know that your act might be more entertaining to adults than to children, cater to the board's desires. They have a lot of money to spend. A thousand dollars for four or five days' work is as good a reason as any to cater to kids, don't you think?

Board members of the fair usually meet in a state or national convention where they are able to procure a list of names of various entertainers. For the Independent Entertainer, it is difficult to get on such lists. Your best bet is to develop a friendly relationship during the year with an individual member of the fair board. When booking time arrives, you can hopefully persuade that member to influence other board members to see that you are the one they need.

CHARITY WORK: SENIOR CITIZENS AND HOSPITALS

Retirement homes, convalescent centers, and hospitals (especially the children's ward) are always anxious to have someone perform for free. Beginners should make use of this opportunity. The administrative staffs at such establishments are always very friendly and will usually bend over backwards to help you in any way they can. And the audience is always genuinely thankful and appreciative. Parents and other relatives and friends of audience members will hear positive things about you, and may, at some future date, find a way to return the favor.

Be careful to keep clear in your mind the differences between charity work and working for free. These two very different areas can be confusing to separate for the beginner.

HAPPY BIRTHDAY PARTIES!

The best present a parent can give to his young child on his birthday is a successful live entertainment show. For children up to about eight years old, the best choice of performer is a clown. As the child gets older, he and his friends will be able to better appreciate other types of entertainment. In fact, the older they get, the more they dislike clowns.

The usual way of making a sale is by word of mouth. You can try leaving posters and cards hanging in toy stores and bakeries that make birthday cakes, but don't expect much success. I hear very little about entertainers who advertise in this manner. Probably these people are amateurs who expect some lazy advertising to bring in business. Advertising is no substitute for good personal promotion and word of mouth.

Performing at adult birthday parties is also an option to pursue. Avoid getting into situations where you are performing for a gag, though. Clowns especially have to keep an eye on this. You want to make jokes, not be one.

HAPPY STOP BIRTHDAY STOP TELEGRAM STOP SERVICE STOP

This is probably the only employment you will find on weekdays between the hours of 9:00 A.M. and 5:00 P.M. If you live in a large city, it's worth your serious promotion. At a large office, what could create a bigger scene for workers than to have a clown deliver a bouquet of balloons or for a juggler to juggle torches?

When arranging the details for this little surprise, you'll need inside help. Someone will have to know exactly when you will be there. This person will see to it that the birthday person won't suddenly step out of the office for a few moments when you're about to arrive. You're also going to have to find out how long you can perform. After all, an office is a place of work. You can usually plan on five to eight minutes for a show.

Even though your show is short and simple, you're going to have to charge your regular fee. You still have to include in your fee transportation time, preparation time, and the time it took you to promote sales and make the business arrangements.

TALENT SHOWS

Talent shows are valauble promotional tools. Don't plan on winning (although it would be nice if you did), but on exposing your act to the buying public. The talent show is the nearest thing there is to an Independent Entertainer showcase theater. People from all sorts of organizations will be on hand to see what kind of local talent is available for use at their upcoming banquets and such.

KIDS' ORGANIZATIONS

After they made kids, they decided to make clubs and organizations to keep the kids occupied. A beneficial side effect is that these organizations can keep you busy. The YMCA, YWCA, Boy Scouts, Girl Scouts, 4-H Club, and countless other local and regional variations will need you to perform at banquets, meetings, and special seminars.

Securing bookings on a regular basis from these organizations will require hustle. Contact the leader of each individual group, not just the city or regional director. When talking to the head of an organization, ask if there are any other youth organizations operating in the area that you don't know about. If there are any, chances are that he or she will know what they are and whom you should contact.

BIG PEOPLE'S ORGANIZATIONS

After the kids grew up, they discovered they still needed clubs and organizations to keep themselves busy. Thus, there are Elks Clubs, Kiwanis Clubs, Shriners, and others, all suitable for you to perform for. When they aren't having banquets (which they have continuously), they are having picnics. While the members of these organizations tend to be middle class, middle age, and conservative, they are also fun-loving and fun to be around. I have had nothing but first-rate experiences with such clubs. Besides being friendly, they pay fairly. Frequently, they take up donations and give me a little extra tip, something that never happens in other situations (except when my hat is out).

CHURCHES

Performing for church groups? You bet. These groups are constantly in search of "clean and wholesome" entertainment that isn't deathly boring and bland. Independent Entertainment is essentially clean and respectable, and, unless you're really bad, inherently interesting.

Besides performing at church banquets and picnics, you can, if you are so inclined, create shows with a special religious tone and message for presentation at prayer meetings, Bible study groups, and children's classes. Churches are literally starving for this type of entertainment and lesson combination. The few groups and individuals whom I have seen perform in such situations have been bad, bad, bad. Plenty of Spirit, but no skill.

After performing for several churches in a region, it could be possible to develop some relationships that might lead to extended touring through the country for one, or maybe two, denominations. Church headquarters will do your booking and most of the other arrangements that are necessary. Whatever your spiritual reward for performing might be, see to it that your financial reward is as large as possible. I've seen too many church performers who are terribly abused and used by officials who persuade them to perform for token fees. Don't let church officials tell you they have no money to spare. More than likely, they have no money they *want* to spare. The minister and other church officials don't work for free, and neither should you.

THE THEATER LOBBY

Theaters frequently like to have something which will amuse the audience while they are waiting in the lobby for the play to begin. This is more often the case in children's theater than adult theater.

These performances may be formal, where everyone watches your show and applauds at the end, or, they may be casual, allowing people to stroll by, sip a drink, and chit-chat while watching you out of the corner of their eyes. You may perform only on opening night, or for the entire run.

POLITICAL BENEFITS AND OTHER RELATED ENTANGLEMENTS

Why create problems for yourself? If you want to do charity work, perform for the sick and the old. If you have messages and causes you want to spread through the world, do it with your act for the general public. You will accomplish nothing by performing for political benefits, rallies, and the like. You will only associate yourself with a group that other potential buyers might dislike.

I was once invited to perform at a benefit for a political cause on which I was neutral. I wasn't doing anything else that evening, and I wanted to hear the band that would be playing there, so I decided to accept. My only request was that my name not be used in what was to be heavy radio advertising. However, the day before the show, I kept hearing on the radio that I would be performing. More than mildly irritated, I didn't show up at the benefit.

But that was not the end of it. For months afterward, people would confront me and demand to know how I could support such a cause. Other people would slap me on the back with a "Hey, fellow brother!" I was associated with something that wasn't me. Even if I had been in favor of the cause, it still wouldn't be a good thing. I lost, for a while, my independence. Audiences and buyers didn't see me as an Independent Entertainer—they saw me as one of *them*, or as one of *us*. Nobody saw me as *me*.

That's the total avoidance side of the story. There's also the total commitment side of the story: creating a show designed specifically for use at political meetings, rallies, and benefits. I have seen a few antinuclear power puppet shows that travel through the country and work in conjunction with antinuke chapters. These shows have always been nice, tight, one-man performances. Another variation is designing a custom-made show on request. For example, you might create a puppet show on the virtues and importance of voting for the League of Women Voters.

ELEMENTARY SCHOOLS

The best way to work elementary schools, especially for beginners, is to perform separately for each classroom, not at a mass assembly. This gives you the opportunity to be informal and conversant with the children, and give short, tight shows that won't bore them. You might give as many as sixteen different performances at a school.

Arranging these shows is either a pain in the neck or a piece of cake. There seems to be little middle ground. First, contact the principal—not the principal's secretary, not the vice principal, but the principal. If this administrator is on-the-ball, he or she will listen to your plan, realize it can't be beat, and "You got the job—we'll be waiting for you." If the principal is a dyed-in-the-wool administrator, you'll be told, "Now just a minute, young man, have you okayed this with the district superintendent? Maybe I should discuss this with some of the teachers. Perhaps I should get approval at the next board meeting. We'll get back to you on this, young man. Thank you." Don't expect him or her to get back to you, and don't waste any more time with this thankless public official. You can perform a hundred other shows by the time you get in touch with the superintendent or until the next board meeting. Don't let yourself, an Independent Entertainer, get caught in the lairs of bureaucracy.

Getting paid for school performances is tricky. You'll need the principal to help you. Chances are extremely remote that the school will have the extra funds to pay you, so the money will have to come from eslewhere. The principal might go to the PTA and succeed, but PTAs tend to move slowly—meetings, discussions, votes, more talk, allocation of surplus funds, etc. It's far better to contact a Dad's Club (if the school has any) or other similar informal, fact-acting organization. ("Yeah, I'll throw in five bucks and Eddy'll pop for ten or so, and so will Bob. We'll have the money for you tomorrow.")

For the most part, don't plan on being paid for performances in public elementary school. Consider it a learning and promotional performance.

JUNIOR HIGH AND HIGH SCHOOL

Don't waste your time. These kids are too busy learning to be cool and adult to give you the attention and consideration you want. You might try performing at an assembly, but generally the school officials will only consider you if you are affiliated with a nationally known assembly booking organization. Bureaucrats feel more important when they can deal with big businesses instead of local, independent hustlers.

NURSERY SCHOOLS

As a clown, I've always had good luck receiving a fair payment for performing at nursery schools. Since they are usually private operations, they know that keeping the kids happy will keep the tuition-paying parents happy.

Make sure the buyer knows there is no guarantee regarding audience response. These children are still young and unpredictable. I once performed before a group of children who watched me for about eighteen seconds before they went back to more important things like running around crazy and screaming their lungs out. They didn't even want to touch my nose, which really upset me. I was paid by the director, who wore a silent, disgruntled face. The door was slammed behind me. You win some and you lose some.

FRATERNITIES AND SORORITIES

These are not always the greatest audiences, but when they happen to have some money left over from the last kegger, they'll enjoy spending it on something different and fun. Most colleges and universities have a central "Greek" office where you can get the names and numbers of the various house activity directors. You should be able to earn top dollar.

DORMITORIES

Some college dormitories have a regular entertainment program. Those that don't can frequently be convinced to schedule a special event. Don't expect to earn more than a minimal fee. Contact the student housing office at the college for the names and numbers of the head residents or the activity coordinators. They are usually very friendly and appreciative of your efforts.

HALF-TIME SHOWS

I once performed a juggling act at the half-time show of a major university basketball game. I made the mistake of not rehearsing at the court, making it more difficult than I imagined it would be to adapt to the lights, the huge empty space of the basketball arena and the distant ten thousand spectators. I dropped more props than usual but still was successful. One thing I had going for me was that I was a very unusual half-time show for an audience that was accustomed to a display of school bands and majorettes.

Schedule half-time performances months in advance. Your income will probably be derived from a local merchant who will sponsor you in return for a quick ad on the public address system. If the athletic department's promotional director is lazy, you'll have to hustle the sponsorship on your own. You should earn a large sum of money for this type of performance.

CONVENTIONS

Informal trade conventions offer the best opportinities for work. The convention directors are looking for something more fun and sparkly than tractors and copying machines, both for the business-minded adults and the restless children. Most convention committees have an entertainment or public relations director whom you could contact. If they don't, it's probably too small of a convention to make use of your services. As with large half-time shows, plan on earning big dollars.

LINES OF PEOPLE

Movie theaters, concerts, and plays are all likely to have lines of people waiting outside. These people are in the mood to be entertained. They are also likely to be bored and frustrated with waiting, making your appearance welcome. I was once paid by the owner of four theater cinemas to entertain the lines of people so they would be less irritated with the theater management.

There are two basic types of lines: stationary and moving.

If the line is stationary, you'll actively have to solicit donations. At the end of your act, it's good to make a little speech about the virtues of donations, allowing your audience a moment to dig out change. Start at the beginning of the line and move toward the end. Don't be pushy. If they don't have their money out when you approach, they won't dig it out when you give them a pleading or belligerent line.

If the line is moving, you can perform at the front with your donation hat placed behind you. It's a good idea to put the hat on a coat or other soft material—people will often throw money and miss the hat, letting the coins bounce and roll into gutters and other undesirable places.

Some performers have a circuit of lines that they "hit." In one evening it's possible to hit a dozen lines and bring in over two hundred dollars. Of course, for every good night, there's at least one bad night, not to mention rain, snow, howling winds, and the risk of being mugged.

GRAND OPENINGS, SALES, AND OTHER PROMOTIONAL WORK

Your main purpose in being employed at grand openings and sales is to entice parents to bring their children. Hopefully, once the parents are there, they'll buy whatever the store is selling. With good advertising, this gambit works. Without good advertising, you will merely entertain those who already had decided to attend the sale. This is also a good thing for your employer, who will now have even happier customers with happier memories of his establishment. In any event, don't forget to remind your employer when approaching him or her for the job that your services are tax deductible.

To line up jobs, you've got to be one step ahead of the game. Don't wait to learn of sales by watching the newspapers—keep in constant touch with businesses to find out what their plans are. It's smart to check with them once a month.

You've also got to convince the businessperson that your performance will realize a profit for him, either in the long or short term. Companies aren't in business to give things away, including your performance.

STILTS

One incredibly amazing form of promotional work, especially for clowns, is tromping on stilts through the downtown streets. People cannot disregard your presence when you wear them. They will watch you in awe, listen to you, follow you to your sponsor's establishment and remember you. If you are ever out of work, drag out your stilts and *someone* will pay you to walk through town exhorting the virtues of his or her business.

Stilts are surprisingly easy to learn to use. You can buy them or make your own. While they are more dangerous because you can't jump off of them, make the kind that strap to your legs. Have someone make you an extra long pair of pants to wear that create the illusion of long legs.

I would have mentioned stilts under "Clown Props" in Chapter 2 if it weren't for the fact that stilt work is such a unique and profitable area of employment for the Independent Entertainer. I suggest that clowns develop a different character, look, and name for stilt work. Other Independent Entertainers will find stilt work, as a clown, easy to pursue and develop. All you have to do is make the stilts, the costume, learn to walk safely (a matter of a short hour or two), and develop a friendly personality. You don't even need to buy a stilt-walking license from the government.

TELEVISION COMMERCIALS

Naturally, you will be quite honored when approached by advertisers to appear in a television commercial. Don't let this get in the way of business. I've known a few Independent Entertainers who were taken advantage of and even cheated by advertising and filming companies. The less money they pay you, the more they keep.

While your fee will vary according to the size of the local market, you should collect at least twenty-five to thrity dollars an hour. You should also collect a residual fee for each time the commercial is run. Don't settle for less than one dollar per showing—try for two or three. To guarantee your residuals, sign a contract with the business for whom you are advertising, not with the company shooting the commercial. Once the filming company has shot the commercial, they're through with it.

If your commercials are so successful that the advertising company or the advertiser decides to come back to you, double or triple your fee. The advertiser might easily be spending as much as a hundred dollars per showing of the commercial, so your fee won't be considered any more than a drop in the bucket.

PIZZA AND ICE CREAM PARLORS

It's almost as though pizza and ice cream parlors were specifically designed for the Independent Entertainer. The seating and table arrangement is very open, conducive to a group feeling that makes for a better audience, and the people that eat there do so because they're looking for a relaxed, informal situation where they can have exuberant fun and make a little noise. They are *ready!*

The management knows that entertainment would be nice. This makes it easy to develop a regular, weekly performance schedule. Some entertainers work six and seven nights a week for months and months.

Don't be too demanding of your audience. They may not want to stop their conversations to watch your performance, only catching glimpses of you now and then. Other times everyone will stop everything, even eating, to watch and listen to you. Never knowing what to expect from night to night, you've got to be able to give both silent and talking routines.

If you encounter a noisy group, don't get riled or feel like an intruder crying for attention. Work at individual tables, especially those with children at them.

In addition to your regular pay, you may receive tips from the audience. Since passing the hat in a restaurant is really too aggressive and presumptuous, I leave a shoe or cigar box at the cash register that has a little sign on it saying "For the Clown" or whatever I happen to be that night. When people are at the cash register paying for their meal, it's easy for them to drop that extra quarter or two into the box.

YOUR OWN PRODUCTION

After your initial gush of success, you'll be tempted to produce your own show. If you want to do this merely to satisfy your ego, go ahead and do it first class and have fun. If you are thinking of producing a show to earn money think twice.

You'll have to rent a hall or a theater. These don't come cheap. You'll have to decide on a date—and hope a circus or traveling stage show or big basketball game or snowstorm doesn't come through town that same day. You'll have to decide on the number of shows you're going to perform and their length. You'll have to pay for advertising. Besides the newspaper, you'll want to print posters, which you'll be responsible for posting and taking down. You'll need someone to take the admission fee from people—can you trust this person not to slip an extra ten into his pocket? Have you seen to it that he or she has the right amount of change? Are you going to work with other entertainers besides yourself? How much will you pay them?

These are only a few of the details you'll have to attend to in producing a show. As mentioned in the chapter on puppets, your enthusiasm will encourage you to take on more than you can handle. If your noble dreams and valiant efforts don't end in disaster, they won't do much better than help you break even. I have seen dozens of good, intelligent, hardworking Independent Entertainers try their hand at promoting, only quietly, sadly, and miserably to fail. Even if you do show a profit on money invested, it won't be enough to cover all the hours you've spent on promoting, planning, and scheduling, not to mention the worries involved with the big gamble of your money. You'll earn more money per hour by performing on the streets without any of the headaches and frustrations.

If you still insist on producing your own show, at least start out as small as possible. Keep your capital investments at a minimum, if not at zero. Plan only on breaking even with your first few efforts. Do free promotional shows in the schools, and find a local merchant who'll rent a room or hall to you in exchange for advertisement and public relations.

TEACHING: THE NON-PERFORMING SOURCE OF INCOME

Teaching your skills to others completes your process of learning. Beyond increasing the skills and knowledge of others, you teach yourself. In responding to student questions and by being a responsible teacher, you'll be forced to think and verbalize the *why* of everything you teach. You'll frequently find yourself thinking "Hmm, now why *do* I do that? Why should they do it?" Teaching will serve as a formalized and intensive form of analysis of your own skills and knowledge.

Teaching also affords you the opportunity to discuss intelligently with genuinely interested people (they're expending effort and maybe money to take your class, aren't they?) the skills and art you are teaching. The first Independent Entertainment class I taught was juggling. After each class, my students and I would spend at least an hour discussing and creating theories and analyses of different aspects of juggling. Representing diverse backgrounds (computer science, modern dance, psychology, teaching, and others), these students offered information and ideas that were invaluable to me in developing respect and perspective toward juggling and Independent Entertainment. This has been the case with every other Independent Entertainment class I have taught.

In addition to what you'll be forced to learn about yourself and your art, you'll aslo gain prestige and financial profit from teaching. "Say, aren't you the guy who teaches puppetry through the university Outreach Program? Why don't you perform for our group?" You are no longer, in many eyes, a guy out to make a buck—you are now a dedicated artist associated with a respected, venerable institution: education.

PLACES TO TEACH

The best place to teach is through an alternative education program associated with a university or college. These programs are not only prestigious, they are backed by money and people that will advertise your class, enroll students, and find a room for your use. Potential students will turn first to these programs when looking for the sort of classes you'll teach.

Other programs to teach through include the YMCA, various camps, and adult education.

Student tuition and teacher payment vary from program to program. Some programs will expect you to teach for free, while others will pay you as much as thrity dollars an hour. You should try to charge as much as the market will bear.

Some programs will allow you to collect the tuition fee directly from the students. The program will either charge the students a registration fee or collect a percentage from you to help cover its costs. Others will collect the fee from the students and pay you either a salary or give you the tuition fee in the form of a salary at the end of the course.

Some performers, especially jugglers, give private lessons. I have heard of street jugglers who, after giving a show, will teach people how to juggle for a five- or ten-dollar fee. The course fee usually includes a set of bean bags.

"WHERE ELSE CAN I WORK?"

The book has by no means included a finite listing of places to perform. For the Independent Entertainer, the only limit is imagination. The hungier are are, the more possibilities you'll discover. I've performed at a welder's festival, in airplanes, trains, inside of movie theaters before the movie began, at laundromats, and for restaurant waitresses and cooks (in exchange for a meal). Where else to perform? Wherever you can.

9.
Business Matters

Financial success in the entertainment world is no accident. It is the result of hard work and careful business management combined with at least some talent.

Study and follow the guidelines suggested in this chapter. It will save you many dollars in lost sales and prevent many hours being wasted on inefficient, unnecessary practices. Most importantly, these practices will allow you to deal with the business aspect of Independent Entertainment with confidence and a minimum of worry, allowing you to spend more time and energy on the creative aspects.

KEEP THOSE RECORDS TIDY AND UP-TO-DATE

The Date Book If it only saves you from missing one scheduled performance, your date book will more than pay for itself. I suggest carrying a pocket-sized date book with you at all times. Don't take the chance of writing down on a paper napkin the date, place and time for a performance two months in the future. Write down all such information in your date book. It's also convenient to list scheduled performances on a large calender at home.

The date book also serves as a record of your work. In mine, I write down how many hours were involved in the total show (transportation, set up, performance, tear down, and hang time), what I was paid, the number of people in the audience, and the general success of the show.

Ledger You can buy a small ledger for a few dollars. It is used to keep a careful record of your income and expenses. In my ledger, I have columns for the date of the transfer, the object transferred, the income and expenses. At the end of each month, I compare the income total with the expense total to determine my profit.

This ledger should be kept up-to-date. Your ledger will reveal quite clearly the degree of your financial success, leaving no room for wishful thinking and fanciful distortions.

Receipts All receipts should be kept in an envelope with your ledger. Should the tax man ever come a knockin', you'll need to show him every one of them (and will probably wish you had more).

Contracts When finalizing an agreement for a performance, it can be useful to have some contracts on hand—one for the buyers and one for the seller. The contract should include the place of performance; its time, date, and length; the buyer; the seller; the fee; and when the fee is to be paid.

I always use a contract when large amounts of money and time are involved, and when the character of the buyer is questionable. As a rule, though, contracts are seldom used in Independent Entertainment.

Listing of Clients and Potential Clients Whenever you do a performance, write down the name, phone number, and address of the person with whom you made the arrangements in a special list. Likewise, write down the names of potential customers with whom you've come in contact or have heard of. In the future, these people are easily contacted.

Idea Journal This is an optional piece of stationary, but one that you will find quite useful. In my journal, I write down every skit and routine I perform. I also write down routines I'd like to do in the future, even if I only have a vague idea of what it might be. This way, I never have to worry about forgetting anything. You may write down a vague idea that you can't seem to develop, only to look at it a year later and have all sorts of ideas flood into your brain.

PROMOTIONAL MATERIAL

The Portfolio Your most important piece of promotional material is your portfolio, usually in the form of a photograph album. It serves the function of a scrapbook, too. It should contain photographs from your first performances up to your most recent, along with photos of the audiences and their smiling faces, and the places at which you've performed. Also include any newspaper articles ever written about you, along with advertisements bearing your name. Even letters of recommendation and thanks should be put in the portfolio for people to read.

The growth of your portfolio will be slow but consistent. Keep it up-to-date. Get pictures taken and put them in, even if they're now award winners. Potential customers mostly want proof that you've actually performed. After free performances at schools and hospitals, strongly suggest that someone write you a letter of thanks and recommendation. If they want to see you perform again for free, they'll be happy to write anything you want.

If a potential customer hasn't seen you perform, your portfolio will often make the sale. It will serve to back up your own charming self with some evidence of previous experience and success.

Business Cards Be frugal. Don't worry about creating a slick, expensive look. All you need is something simple and clean that conveys the necessary information: your name, phone number, address, functions and groups you have performed for, and the essentials of your act.

You might find it helpful to use a post office box for the business address on your card. Many Independent Entertainers frequently change residences. It's awkward to scratch out the old address and write in the new one. It's also expensive to buy new cards merely to update the address.

Publicity Photos For the purpose of newspaper advertisements and posters, you may want to have a standard publicity photo. Contact a professional photographer. He'll provide you with a photo that has maximum reproduction quality in mass-produced form.

Posters, Flyers, Handbills I avoid using this form of advertisement. It always tends to look cheap and amateurish. The paper is always crinkled up by the recipient and often ends up littering the streets. I think it produces more of a negative than positive impression. I've never seen top-quality, successful Independent Entertainers resort to this form of advertising.

Telephone Book Advertisements This is one option of promotion, or rather, advertisement, that I haven't yet pursued. It's expensive, but then, only a few performances would pay for it. I suggest listing your ad in the talent agency section. Such promotion might work very well, especially if you are able to perform a number of different acts. Let's face it, when someone wants to hire a juggler or a magician, where does that person find one if he doesn't know of any? The phone book seems the logical place to start.

MASS MEDIA AND THE INDEPENDENT ENTERTAINER

Newspapers Most of your dealings with the mass media will be through the newspapers. You each have something to offer the other. The paper will provide you with free advertisement and you will provide the paper with an interesting feature story and photographs.

While I have generally benefited from articles in newspapers, I have had some problems in dealing with people on the staffs. They tend to abuse the mistaken viewpoint that the subjects for articles need the paper more than the paper needs them. They become rude and inconsiderate with their sense of self-importance. More than once I've walked into a class I was teaching only to find bright lights, extension cords, photographers, and writers sprawled all over the room and interfering with my students—without my previous knowledge or consent! It's as though the purpose of the classes was to provide the paper with something to write about.

The only way to stay ahead of the press is to be aggressive. Get in touch with them early in your career, before they have a chance to find out about you on their own. Notify them that you'd like them to do some sort of story on you. Be forward and direct. First get in touch with the feature editor. After that, speak separately to the feature writers and photographers. Make sure each of them knows who you are and what you are interested in, and that you wish to be notified ahead of time as to when they would like to interview you and take photographs. That way, you can be sure to have some interesting quotes prepared and be wearing photogenic clothing.

Journalists will generally write a very shallow story on your act that concentrates on the sensational— "Juggler Juggles Five Bean Bags and Bowling Ball!" They'll totally ignore your comments that describe your juggling to be unique because it was inspired by and developed upon the theories of modern abstract art and dance.

Unless you know that an interviewer will write an intelligent, honest article, play it safe. Give only the basic information that you think will help your career and that can't be distorted too much. Don't speak about things that can be easily confused or forgotten. Concentrate on what is unique about your act, how much the audience always enjoys it, and your future plans. And don't forget to mention how people can get in touch with you.

Don't get too worked up over an article when it comes out. At best, readers will remember your name and what you do. Unlike you, they will register little of the information, correct or distorted.

Pursue the writing of articles and the inclusion of photographs in all available newspapers: city, college, and high school. When travelling, plan performances solely for various city papers to do stories on. Nothing looks better than a portfolio of articles from around the country.

Television The smaller the television station, the more likely it is you'll appear on it. You can easily appear as a feature story on the local news show, or as a guest on a morning or afternoon talk show. Like newspaper editors, television producers are always looking for an interesting story or guest. An Independent Entertainer is particularly desirable because he is visually interesting, not just another talking head.

SALES AND SELLING

Clothing manufacturers know that the average person will buy, let's say, eight pairs of pants per year. The only thing their salespeople have to do is persuade buyers which pants to buy. But the Independent Entertainer has no idea how many performances will be "purchased" during a year. Customers have no idea either. You'll never hear, "I've got to pick up some groceries, get the car from the mechanic, and schedule our next entertainment act." You are not a necessity, not even a regularly considered luxury. This means you are faced with the task of creating your own market. Because of this, you are going to have to be thorough and professional in your salesmanship. You are going to have to make that extra effort that salespersons in dependable, predictable markets don't have to make.

ETERNAL HUSTLE AND BLIND CONFIDENCE

Don't even bother thinking about the odds against success. Believe that you will succeed, and that's all there is to it. There is no room for discussion. Success requires constant, never-ending effort and hustle. But you knew that before you got into this business, didn't you?

PERSONAL CONTACT

You will rely more on personal contact to make sales than any other method. If people can see your face, see that you have a responsible appearance, nice manners, and that you express optimism and confidence, they'll feel good about being with you. That means they are likely to think audiences will feel good about being with you, too.

Whenever possible, talk to people in person. Avoid the telephone. Don't write letters. Forget about posters. Don't wait for word-of-mouth from your charity performances to bring in business. Get out and meet people, talk and laugh with them, discuss business, shake a lot of hands. Follow this course of action with everyone, not just the immediately potential customer. Sooner or later—sooner than you would think, too—word will spread: "Hey, I know a guy who'd be great for your kid's birthday party next month. I met this really nice, friendly guy who does these puppet shows—have I seen the shows? No, but they gotta be first-rate. I mean, this guy is on the ball...."

ALWAYS BUSY AND SUCCESSFUL

Even when you're hungry and haven't performed since who knows when, don't let buyers know. ("If this guy's down on his luck, maybe he isn't so good." Make them think you're so busy and successful, they're lucky you're even bothering with them. ("We can't go wrong picking a winner.") This advice may sound simplistic and cliché, but it works. Use it to your advantage.

TAKE ME TO YOUR LEADER

The only person to whom you should present a business proposition is the owner of an establishment. Do not explain your proposition to underlings so that they may relay the information— never once have I succeeded in getting a job with this approach. The message either gets distorted or the owner doesn't have the chance to see that you are a professional, not a slob out to make an easy buck.

I cannot stress enough that you are asking for failure if you don't talk to the owner.

USING THE TELEPHONE

The larger the organization you wish to perform for, the more difficult it becomes personally to make the initial contact with the owner. This is when to use the telephone.

When using the telephone, it is best to have an exact idea of what you want to do for the organization and present that plan to the person in charge. He might think something else is better, but he'll also see that you are thoughtful and mean business. Do not suggest that you are "interested in doing some kind of a magic show sometime in the future." If you do, he'll lie to you when he says he'll take your name and get back to you in the future.

LETTERS

Even larger organizations, especially those that are located a long distance away from you, are best contacted through the mail. These organizations are efficient. Your letter will be answered. If the answer is positive, pursue as indicated. If not, forget it.

Do not mention fees in introductory letters, only a description of yourself and your act. Also mention what you think you can accomplish for that organization.

WALKING THE STREETS

"Walking the streets" implies an intense business-getting effort among Independent Entertainers. This is a common practice for beginners, as well as for more experienced entertainers who find their regular business slacking off.

Armed with your portfolio and a smile, set off early in the morning. At the end of the day, you may have visited as many as fifty business establishments and talked to the owners or arranged another time to talk to them. The owners now know who you are, what your act is, how it can be used to their advantage, and how they can get in contact with you. Out of fifty establishments, you can bet that at least half a dozen are planning some kind of sale in which they could include your skills.

Walking the streets is tiring and frustrating. It is, however, one of the surest ways available to get your message directly to those who might be interested.

AGENTS

The only time you will have need of an agent is when you begin to move out of the area of Independent Entertainment and into the big time. There are some Independent Entertainers who try to make use of local or regional booking agents who are responsible for booking small bands at high schools and parties. Since these agents don't stand to earn very much from your act in commissions, they're going to push you as hard as the more profitable acts. Don't waste your time or theirs. Do your own booking.

COLLECTING FEES

The very best time (and the most customary) to collect your fee is immediately after a performance. You will save yourself many worries by seeing that your employer pays you at this time. If you have to go back at another time to pick up your pay, you're making an extra trip, plus, son of a gun and whaddya know, the guy just happened to slip out the door for a few minutes before you drove up. After waiting an hour, you leave the message that you'll come back later. He can leave the money in an envelope. Now you have to make *another* trip plus hope he got the message and that he follows through on it. My own record is seven trips to collect money owed me.

Get your money *now!* Don't let people put you off. You can't afford to give credit. One of the stunts employers like to pull, if they have employees, is to have you wait for a check in the mail that they make out at the same time they do the payroll. Sorry, you inform them, you are not an employee, you are contract labor and you need to be paid *now.*

You are a very small, one-man independent business, the easiest kind to be abused and cheated by those who are out for the fast and dirty dollar. You are a prime target. Exercise caution and don't be the least bit afraid to seem pushy or aggressive in demanding *your* money *now.*

SEASONAL ASPECTS

The smaller the city you work in, the more likely you will find it more efficient to operate on a seasonal basis. Concentrate your efforts, on a full-time basis, to one or two seasons of the year. This prevents you from suffering the ailments of frustration and low annual income. Frsutration results because overexposure brings less jobs per month than you need to keep yourself feeling active. Less income results because small-town merchants, knowing they can have your services at any time, don't consider your act as special or as valuable as they might otherwise. They'll pay in accordance with the value they place on your services.

The other seasonal aspect to consider is the weather. Fortunately, seasons nicely balance out the workload for the Independent Entertainer. Warm seasons permit you to do more outside work, and cold seasons usually call for increased indoor work.

KEEP THE CUSTOMER SATISFIED

Unhappy customers are a twofold loss. First, they aren't likely to rehire you. Second, they are liable to inform others of their dissatisfaction. To keep customers happy, make sure both you and they know exactly what they want and what they are going to get. If you provide this information, at least they can't accuse you of shirking your responsibilities. If a show doesn't work, talk to your employer and discuss what went wrong and what can be done in the future to make it better. The customer should be smart enough to forsee the problems, especially any obvious ones (everyone in town may have been at the big football game). Just to show you're a great guy who wants everyone to come out ahead, volunteer to do an extra little show for your employer at no charge. If that doesn't knock the customer for a loop and make you more appreciated, nothing will. Do not offer to cut the price of your show; for some reason, people respond better to freebies than to discounts.

Always do a little something extra for your customers. They will appreciate and remember it for years to come, much to the advantage of your pocketbook.

DETERMINING FEES

Always charge as much as you possibly can. You're in the entertainment field to entertain, but you're in the entertainment *business* to make money. Make as much today as you possibly can. Tomorrow you may not be able to make any money at all.

Some very general figures that I hear tossed around among Independent Entertainers run anywhere from twenty-five to fifty dollars per show as a minimum charge. They try to get more when possible. A show may include several performances, too. The more successful clowns that I have known charge at least fifty dollars an hour for performance time. For teaching classes, a minimum rate is generally ten dollars an hour.

These figures are not to be followed blindly. They are merely approximate averages. There are many variables to be considered that will change the prices you charge from show to show. How wealthy is the family that hired you for the birthday party show? How many people will be in attendance at the Elks banquet? Will you be performing regularly for another year at the pizza parlor, or is it for just this one night? Are you flat broke and hungry? Is this one of your first shows? Was your picture on the front page of last night's paper? Is your telephone ringing day and night with requests and invitations?

When proposing a price to a potential customer, remember this: It is easy to lower your price, impossible to raise it. Start out high. If he balks, come down. If not, you're money ahead.

THE VIRTUES OF BARTERING

As I suggested earlier, barter your talents in exchange for products and services. This form of exchange will increase your chances of working for small businesses that don't have the capital to spend on luxury promotions. Shoemakers, photographers, and printers are all likely business people from whom you could profit by bartering.

MAINTAIN A MINIMUM OUTLAY AND OVERHEAD

Analyze carefully the financial profits your investments and operational expenditures are returning. Try to operate with the lowest possible capital outlay and overhead.

One of the easiest ways for an Independent Entertainer to lower his profit is to spend more than he absolutely needs to spend. Must you spend fifty dollars on a costume when you can spend as little as twenty dollars for essentially the same thing? Does your answering service bring in extra business? Do you have to spend another one hundred fifty dollars on a new puppet stage? Can't you get by without a three-color business card?

Once you have established your act and begin to book performances on a regular basis, I doubt strongly that increased expenditures will increase your income. Before letting any money out of your hand, be absolutely certain the object or service you're buying will either bring in more jobs or will allow you to operate with significantly more speed or efficiency.

SETTING FINANCIAL GOALS

I have always found it extremely helpful and satisfying to set monthly financial goals. Rather than approach a vague, open-ended financial future, I have an attainable destination. Attempting to reach this goal provides impetus to hustle hard and keep my eyes open for performance possibilities. You will be surprised to see how much money you can earn when you really apply yourself. If you plan on only earning enough to pay the bills, that's probably all you'll earn, if that much.

Independent Entertainment is a business that hasn't been fully explored. The only limits are those that you set for yourself. Create and fulfill your own standards for success.

ESTABLISHING FINANCIAL CREDIT

Not unlike most people, there will come a time when you'll want to buy a new car or home and to do so you'll need to borrow money from a financial institution. If Independent Entertainment is to be your sole source of income, it will be tough for you to establish credit. Some day when you've got an extra hour or two, talk to the credit people at your bank about your situation. And while you're there, see if they'll sponsor you in the upcoming parade.

SIMULTANEOUS WORK IN NONINDEPENDENT ENTERTAINMENT JOBS

Most Independent Entertainers, because of a wide variety of reasons, will not earn quite enough income from Independent Entertainment to keep themselves happy. These people will look elsewhere for additional income. If you wish to work at other jobs and still maintain the maximum amount of time for performing, schedule your work carefully. Working mornings and early afternoons on weekdays will probably interfere very little with your performing. Getting off early in the afternoons allows you to hustle up work during normal business hours, too.

The best nonindependent entertainment jobs are those that allow you to meet the public, because these jobs allow you to plug yourself to potential customers. If possible, stay away from jobs that are physically tiring. It's hard to be cheery and make silly jokes when you are completely exhausted.

10.
You, Independent Entertainment and the Rest of the World

THE OTHER INDEPENDENT ENTERTAINERS

It's bad enough that your career is a difficult, bumpy, unpredictable one at best. To top things off, *he* has to come along. *He* can juggle seven balls, for crying out loud! And you can't even begin to figure out his magic tricks.

Competition. Yuk. I don't care what they say about the potential of competition to sharpen your talent. It puts a crimp in your already-not-too-fat pocketbook, especially if you live in a small town.

Since you aren't likely to drive your competition out of business (he may be performing as a hobby), your best approach to the problem is to ignore it. Continue doing what you think is your best performing for a fee that you consider to be fair. If you've got a good act that audiences enjoy, don't try to change it to be competitive. Don't let others dictate the substance of your act. Especially, don't try to be financially competitive. Stick to your guns. Don't worry about what the other guy charges; there's always someone who'll provide a service or product for less money than the next guy.

Beyond the financial woes, it's a drag listening to people talk about how great another Independent Entertainer is. And you can't complain about him or criticize, of course. People will think you are an insecure, jealous, spiteful person. And you're not. You just don't ... particularly ... like ... OTHER ... COMPETITORS ... RAINING ON YOUR PARADE!!! That's all. But hey, you're not in the least bit insecure, jealous, or spiteful as you patiently listen to people heap adulations on this other performer. ("I just hope this guy's visiting town for a short while and not making it his home!")

"SAY, AREN'T YOU...?"

Eventually, you are going to meet your competition face to face. Hopefully, he'll be as friendly and cordial as you are. If not, he'll probably be one of two other basic types. The first is the arrogant, aloof, quiet type. He obviously considers himself superior to you.

He will say very little. You will say very little to him. Each of you probably wishes to have some talent or skill the other has. Neither of you will admit it. Each of you wishes to think of something to say that will crack the other's sense of confidence. Neither of you can think of anything. You part quickly and do not look forward to the next encounter. You hope against hope that no one will ever again see it their duty to describe in glowing details how great this guy is. You hope even more that he never hears the end of what a wonderful person and entertainer you are.

The other type of competitor is a lot more fun. He doesn't hear a word you say. He's too busy talking about himself and his act. He will tell you, whether or not you want to hear it, how he got started, how much money it's cost him, how much time he's invested, how much he earns, and his plans for the future and precisely how he intends to carry them out. All you have to do is listen and show a little bit of interest to keep him rolling. You'll soon learn everything he knows about Independent Entertainment.

This latter type of competitor is certainly more exciting than the former—he has a lot more energy and vivacity. This makes up for his lack of careful thinking (what careful thinker is going to tell you the details of his business?). But don't underestimate him. His enthusiasm will bring him a good deal of success.

"DAD, I WANT TO GIVE UP MEDICAL SCHOOL. I WANT TO BE A PUPPETEER"

Your decision to pursue Independent Entertainment as a full-time profession will not likely be greeted with applause from your family. They will consider it a phase that you are going through and hope that it will pass soon so that you can move on to something more serious and dependable. Odds are, you know yourself it's only a temporary phase. You only plan to pursue it for a certain amount of time and that's all. That doesn't mean it can't be enjoyed or pursued with confidence or enthusiasm.

Maintain your blind confidence. Your family, while they love you and are proud of you, will try to persuade you to give up your new career sooner than you'd like, or to relegate it to a part-time basis. They will pressure you with hints about security, your future, higher income, and so on. They mean well and certainly have valid points to make—they just don't understand that it's what you really want to do.

Hmmm. Sounds like a problem that parents and their children have had for quite some time, doesn't it?

MIXING SOCIAL LIFE WITH BUSINESS

There's no reason you can't meet people and enjoy social intercourse before or after a performance. As long as you don't neglect talking to and devoting sufficient time to your employer and other prospective customers, no harm is done.

The only times I've encountered any problems is when I've been a "host" for a group of friends or acquaintances. This is most common when I perform at an eating establishment. My guests come to watch me and eat a meal and have a good time. There's a conflict in that *I'm* not there to have a good time, I'm there to conduct business. Seeing that my guests have finished dinner and are impatiently waiting to leave (we have used the same car), I am forced to cut short an important business conversation. Should I continue the conversation, my guests will feel that I am rude and inconsiderate of their concerns (or at least I worry that they are feeling this way).

You will have enough to worry about without the added pressure of entertaining friends. If friends do want to watch you perform, make sure they make plans completely separate of yours. If they don't understand your predicament, that's their problem. You have a business to take care of.

HOW TO WREAK HAVOC ON YOUR ROMANTIC RELATIONSHIP(S)

It starts out with "Gee, honey, why don't you learn to juggle so we can pass clubs together on stage?" It ends with "good-bye!"

Unless your partner was an Independent Entertainer at the time you began your relationship, don't—repeat, *don't*—cajole her into becoming one. I've never once seen it work. What I've seen are divorces and breakups, without exception. Independent Entertainers who are willing to let their partners make their own decisions concerning the entertainment profession tend to have happy, balanced relationships.

Don't push your luck—and don't push your partner. If she *wants* to perform, consider yourself lucky. Even then, proceed with great caution. It can be difficult to work with someone you love, especially in a demanding, high-pressure field.

WOMEN AND SEXISM IN INDEPENDENT ENTERTAINMENT

You've probably noticed that throughout the book I have referred to Independent Entertainers as men. This is done not only because it's easy to use "he" as a generic term, but also because it is rare to find women in the field of Independent Entertainment. They are not a minority, mind you, but a *rarity*. I've only known two women who have operated independently. The few other women in the business operate as limited partners in male-dominated groups, or worse, and even disgustingly, as female assistants whose only value is their body.

Why is it that so very few Independent Entertainers are women? Is it because buyers are sexist when it comes to booking entertainment? I don't think so. Is it because audiences prefer men over women? To some extent, this may be true. Even in the larger commercial world of entertainment, there are more men than women. Still, audience preference is not a valid excuse for the low numbers of women involved in Independent Entertainment.

Perhaps it is because throughout history the Independent Entertainer has traditionally been male. If this is the case, and it seems the most likely, it is time to change tradition. I have yet to hear of a female magician, juggler, or puppeteer operating independently. I know of only one woman mime and one woman clown. It's a sad situation that is good neither for women nor audiences.

Personally, I think a large movement of women into Independent Entertainment would be healthy for the whole profession. It would serve to balance, remove, and positively change many of the often unpleasant male, macho attributes that are accepted as standard in Independent Entertainment. In time, I think it would create a friendlier, more universally appealing standard of excellence.

It seems that Independent Entertainment is waiting, arms open, for women participants. I can see no sexist prejudices within the system, such as it is, that would inhibit the success of women.

HOBBY OR BUSINESS?

After being a full-time professional Independent Entertainer for a period of about two years, I made arrangements to give a performance in a small, casual, not too busy coffee house. Immediately after my performance, two local jazz guitarists were to play music.

I was concerned that my performing conditions be as good as possible. I was very picky. The lights had to be at a certain level. The background music I was using had to be brought in at a particular time and at a proper level. I had to train an employee to do this. I insisted on tables being moved into different positions. I talked to each of the waitresses to make sure they wouldn't walk in front of me or bother customers who were watching. The candles on the dinner tables had to be blown out. I told the cook not to use the microwave oven or the vent fan because the noise would interfere. I told the dishwasher not to clink dishes around. I refused to perform on schedule because I didn't think enough people were in the restaurant at the time to provide the proper atmosphere.

Surprisingly, I had the energy to give a smooth performance.

Then the musicians performed. They were two local fellows who had absolutely no intention of ever turning professional or of even being paid. They only wanted to have fun playing music. And they did. They didn't have to worry about anything but their music, and they had a great time.

For the first time, I realized the distinct differences in approaches to entertainment.

Don't think that I was disappointed in my approach—I wasn't. I did feel a little silly making such a big production out of my fifteen-minute routine in such a relaxed atmosphere, but I considered it an accepted responsibility of being a paid professional. I had chosen that approach.

In developing your own approach to Independent Entertainment, consider carefully the two options of hobby or profession, and possible combinations. Don't let all my talk about earning money and being a professional persuade you to think that this is the most desirable approach. And don't take the previous anecdote to mean a professional can't have fun performing either.

Any approach you develop must first proceed on the basis that you thoroughly enjoy performing. You thrive on showing your juggling skills to people, making them laugh as a clown, deceiving them with your magic tricks, or entertaining them with whatever other types of performing you do. On that basis, you have only to decide how to present those skills to the audience: as a hobbyist or as a professional.

As a hobbyist, you can give more than enough performances to keep you busy in your spare time and even earn a few extra dollars. The money, though, isn't important. You do your act as a form of recreation. Having a good time is your first priority.

As a professional, whether part- or full-time, you'll have a lot more to deal with than the hobbyist. You will be much more concerned with pleasing the audience, hustling up bookings, transportation time, the circumstances of your performances, and the development of a reputation. These worries will add frustration to your work and will certainly distract from the carefree aura associated with entertaining. But then, success as a professional will bring satisfactions that the hobbyist does not experience.

(It should be noted that the difference between, and definition of, hobbyists and professionals is a subjective one. I don't offer strict rules and definitions, only very loose, general ways of thinking which are commonly considered by entertainers of all types.)

REAPING THE NONFINANCIAL BENEFITS OF SUCCESS

After you've gambled your time, energy, and money—and made difficult sacrifices, learned the trade, are able to apply your knowledge intelligently, and can consistently please an audience—there's no reason you can't stand proud with a high degree of confidence in yourself. You've come a long way all on your own and are able to do something very few people in the world can or will ever do.

Relish in this knowledge. *You are a success in one of the most unique, individualistic, independent businesses in the world!*

In and of itself, this knowledge is a wonderful thing in which you can have and take pride. Extend your newfound confidence into realms beyond Independent Entertainment and see what happens. Knowing that you've succeeded in something as admittedly bizarre as Independent Entertainment, other challenges and goals seem easier to meet and attain. To your benefit, other people will sense this confidence. Opportunities will come your way.

POSSIBLE NONINDEPENDENT ENTERTAINMENT FIELDS TO PURSUE

Perhaps you've gotten to the point, or will get to the point, where you've exhausted the potential that Independent Entertainment has to offer. You've given a couple of hundred shows to tens of thousands of people in dozens of different situations, each time with a high degree of success. But it's no longer the thrill for you it once was. Don't regret it when you feel this way. It happens.

In fact, I would go so far as to say it would be abnormal, even sad, if you didn't exhaust the potential of Independent Entertainment within a few years. Intelligent people interested in skills and occupations off the beaten track (and that describes the bulk of

Independent Entertainers) need new and varied challenges to remain happy. So what's next?

One of the common fields of business that is pursued by Independent Entertainers is advertising. This seems to come about from their work at grand openings and sales. Many Independent Entertainers are born promoters.

Besides the advantage of earning a respectable, dependable income, the advertising person is frequently in a position to book his or her own act for clients.

Those who don't go into advertising often go into some kind of sales work where they can employ their stage charm and skills and audience analysis on consumers.

Many employers are anxious to have Independent Entertainers work for them as salespeople, or in other capacities that deal directly with the public. Employers can quickly see that your confidence and experience in dealing with all sorts of peoples can be used to their advantage.

If not in the related worlds of advertising and sales, the only other obvious career choice is in another form of entertainment. During your work as an Independent Entertainer, you'll be in contact with many other types of entertainers. Usually, they'll present themselves to you and start a discussion; they are interested in the unique way you've chosen to entertain. These people can tell you a great deal about their own fields, and maybe even be of help to you in developing contacts and opportunities.

It's difficult, though, for many Independent Entertainers to move into other forms of entertainment when they are only a small part of a larger team. For some, the frustration of not being one's own boss is too great.

For that matter, I've also noticed that Independent Entertainers who have pursued advertising or sales find it difficult to work under an employer. Many ex-Independent Entertainers are either self-employed or would like very much to be that way. It would be interesting to know how much this desire of independence is developed from experience as an Independent Entertainer.

Appendix

The world of Independent Entertainment is rapidly growing. As a result, accessories and services are changing constantly. For instance, while juggling clubs were once constructed in one man's small garage on weekends (ample time for him to supply the entire profession with standard clubs), there are now several large companies working full-time at manufacturing clubs—and some firms with back orders of up to three months.

It would be pointless to offer you a listing of prop sources and publications, since a large number of new books will probably be produced after this book is published, and new companies supplying props and accessories will be formed in the near future to meet the changing needs of a growing profession and hobby.

The best I can do is to provide you with the names and addresses of the largest organizations and clubs involved with Independent Entertainment. Most of them supply a regular newsletter or magazine, sponsor yearly conventions, provide a listing of names and addresses of members, and run advertisements in their magazines for props, accessories, and books. A friendly letter to the organization's administrative offices will usually bring a listing of popular preferred props and books.

Remember that the nature of these organizations is changing, too. In the past decade, membership has risen from a few hundred longtime close professional friends to thousands and thousands of people with a variety of needs and desires. The amateur nature of administration is slowly changing to a professional one. Some organizations have recently folded as a result of the increased pressures of a growing membership. Either the financing wasn't adequate to pay for the necessary full-time positions or the tired old-timers who had run the organization for years didn't want to continue their efforts for a mushrooming pack of neophytes.

These addresses are as current as possible. Often, though, they will change after the annual summer conventions. If your letter isn't forwarded to the new address, I suggest writing to each of the other organizations for current information. They keep in fairly good touch with each other.

The Society of American Magicians
Director of Membership Development
Frank Buslovich
Lock Drawer 789
Lynn, Massachusetts 01903

Clowns of America, Inc.
P.O. Box 3906
Baltimore, Maryland 21222

Puppeteers of America
2015 Novem Drive
Fenton, Missouri 63020

International Jugglers Association
P.O. Box 443
Davidson, North Carolina 28036

WARM REGARDS, AND SO ON

Good luck in your endeavors. I hope this book has been and will continue to be of service to you. At the very least, I hope it has stimulated your interest and caused you to think thoroughly and carefully about all aspects of Independent Entertainment.

I would be honored if you were to write to me and let me know about your career. I'm always eager to hear interesting news from fellow Independent Entertainers. And Independent Entertainers *all* lead exciting, interesting lives. I'm sure yours will be *very* interesting.

Index

Ad libbing, 22
Agents, 128
Amplification in puppetry, 39-40
Apprenticing, 4-5
Assistants, working with, 95-97
Audiences
  avoiding injury to, 80-81
  bombing before, 93-95
  in casual and formal shows, 87-90
  clown's, 21-23
  cramming together of, 90
  expressing opinions to, 85-87
  intermingling with, 97
  involvement of, 22-23, 50
  juggler's, 78-81
  magician's, 59
  mime's, 49-50
  in puppetry, 30, 37-38
  stale acts and, 90-91

Baby-sitting, warning against, 97-98
Balloons, give-away, 23
Balls, juggling, 71-72
Bartering, 130-31
Bean bags, juggling, 71
Beginners
  in clowning, 24
  opportunities for, 101-18
Bible study groups, 107
Birthday parties, 105
Birthday telegrams, 105-6
Bombing, 93-95
Books, instructional, 3
Business cards, 122

Business promotional work, 113
  television commercials, 114
Business records, keeping, 120-21

Candy, giving away, 23
Casual situations, 87-88
Charity performances, 104-5
Chinese stick, 77
Church groups, 107-8
Cigar boxes, juggler's, 76-77
Clients, listing of, 121
Clowning, 9-28
  psychology of, 25, 85
  stilts for, 113-14
Clubs (juggling), 73-75
Clubs (organizations), 107
Cold cream, 15
Commercials, television, 114
Competing with yourself, 102
Competitors, 134-35
Contracts for work, 121
Conventions
  of Independent Entertainers, 3-4
  performing at, 112
Costume
  clown's, 16-20
  juggler's, 77-78
  for magic, 61
  for mimes, 48, 50-51
Credit, establishing, 132
Criticism, making use of, 99

Devil stick, 77, 78
Diabolo, 77

Different acts, ability to perform, 92-93
Discounts on admission prices, 129
Dormitories, performances in, 111

Elementary schools, 109-10
Experience, 6-7
Eyeliner, 14, 51-52

Fairs, 104
Family and career, 135-36
Fawkes, Isaac, 58
Fees, 128-31
Fields, W.C., 77
Fire, juggling, 76
Flyers, 122-23
Formal situations, 88-89
Fraternities, 111
Freebies, 129
Freedom of expression, 85-87
Friends, performing before, 136

Gimmicky magic, 62
Give-away items, 22-23
Grand openings, 113
Grease paint, 13-14, 51

Half time shows, 111-12
Hand puppets, 33-34, 35
Handbills, 122-23
Happy customers, 129-30
Henson, Jim, 30
High schools, 110
Hobby or business? 138-40

Ice cream parlors, 115
Idea journal, 121
In-between situations, 89-90

Jokes
  clown's, 21-22
  for mistakes, 80

Juggler who hands out dollar bills, 101
Juggling, 68-83
Junior high schools, 110

Kids' organizations, 106-7
Kramer, Stanley, 86

Learnings, 2-7, 101
  juggling, 68-69
  magic, 58-59
  mime, 46-47
  puppetry, 30
Ledger, 120
Letters, sales, 127
Licenses for street performing, 102
Lines of people, performing before, 112
Lovers, performing with, 136-37

Magic, 58-66
  mistakes in, 80
Makeup
  for clowning, 10-16
  for mimes, 48, 51-52
Malls, performing in, 103-4
Marionettes, 31-32
Masks in miming, 51
Mime, 46-56
Misdirection in magic, 59-60
Mistakes by jugglers and magicians, 80-81
Mummenschanz Players, 51
Muppets, 30

Name for a clown, 24
Newspapers, stories in, 123-24
Nonindependent entertainment, work in, 132, 140-41
Nursery schools, 110-11

Organizations, performances before, 107

Partners, working with, 95-97
Personal contact in salesmanship, 125-26
Pizza parlors, 89, 97, 115
Places to perform, 101-18
Political events, 85-87, 108-9
Portfolio, 121-22
Prayer meetings, 107
Producing your own show, 115-16
Profession or hobby? 138-40
Profits and expenses, 131
Promotional material, 121-23
Propaganda, see Political events
Props
    clown's, 20-21
    juggler's, 70-77
    magician's, 63
    mime's, 52-53
Publicity photos, 122
Puppetry, 30-44
    political, 30, 38, 109

Recording for puppet shows, 40-42
Receipts for tax purposes, 120-21
Restaurants, shows in, 90
Rings, juggling, 72-73
Rod puppets, 32-33

Sales events, 113
Salesmanship, 125-27
Scarves, juggling, 75-76
Schools, performances in, 109-11
Seasonal aspects, 129
Sexism, 137-38
Sleight-of-hand magic, 62
Smiling, 85
Sororities, 111
Sountracks for puppet shows, 40-42

Sports events, half time shows at, 111-12
Stilts, 113-14
Street entertainment, 102-3

Talent shows, 106
Tax deductibility of entertainer's services, 113
Tax records, 120-21
Teaching your skills, 116-18
Telegrams, birthday, 105-6
Telephone, selling yourself by, 126-27
Telephone book advertisements, 123
Television
    commercials on, 114
    puppetry on, 30
    stories about you on, 124
Theaters
    lines of people at, 112-13
    lobbies of, 108
    renting, 115-16
Threads, see Costume
Title cards, mime's, 53
Torches, juggling, 76
Tuxedos, 61, 78

Variety, 90-91
Versatility, 92-93

Walking the streets, 127
White face, 12, 51
Women in Independent Entertainment, 137-38
Work in Nonindependent entertainment, 132, 140-41

YMCA and YWCA, 106, 117
Yo-yo, 77